# Consumer Contract Legislation
## Understanding the New Law

To Isabella

# Consumer Contract Legislation
## Understanding the New Law

### Geraint Howells LLB

Senior Lecturer, University of Sheffield

BLACKSTONE
PRESS LIMITED

First published in Great Britain 1995 by Blackstone Press Limited,
9-15 Aldine Street, London W12 8AW. Telephone 0181-740 1173

© G. Howells, 1995

ISBN: 1 85431 470 X

British Library Cataloguing in Publication Data
A CIP catalogue record for this book is available from the British Library.

Typeset by Style Photosetting Ltd, Mayfield, East Sussex
Printed by Bell & Bain Ltd, Glasgow

# Contents

## 5   General Product Safety Regulations 1994                          55

Background — EEC Directive — Scope of the changes — 'Producers' and 'distributors' — Products covered — Relationship to vertical regulations — Definition of 'safe product' — Obligations of producers and distributors — New offences — Due diligence defence — Persons liable — Enforcement — Penalties

# Preface

Blackstone Press has developed a reputation for producing good-quality affordable guides to important legislative developments, which appear soon after the laws have been enacted. In other words at the very time when busy business people and lawyers need an easily accessible explanation of the new rules and an assessment of their impact. I was pleased to be involved in an earlier such guide, *Blackstone's Guide to the Food Safety Act 1990* (with R. Bradgate and M. Griffiths). The success of that Guide caused me to approach Blackstone Press again with the present proposal. This is rather unusual in dealing with four pieces of legislation — two statutes (the Sale and Supply of Goods Act 1994 and the Sale of Goods (Amendment) Act 1994) and two sets of Regulations (the Unfair Terms in Consumer Contracts Regulations 1994 and the General Product Safety Regulations 1994). Together the four pieces of legislation have a significant impact on consumer sales law and thus justify the present venture. Indeed the fact that they were enacted separately and without the publicity surrounding a blockbuster Consumer Protection Act may have caused some affected parties to have overlooked the changes or to have underestimated their significance. That some of the legislation is by way of statutory instrument rather than Act of Parliament should not mislead one into underestimating its significance.

The aims of this book are therefore to ensure affected parties are aware of these changes and to explain the nuances of the reforms and how they relate to the existing law. It is hoped that the book is of practical use to those having to grapple with the technical changes in an already complex area of law.

I should mention that many of the insights into the Unfair Terms in Consumer Contracts Regulations 1994 were the result of numerous conversations I had with my colleague Roger Brownsword. Roger and Thomas Wilhelmsson worked with me on an analysis of the Directive which preceded the Regulations and I am indebted to them both, but accept sole responsibility for any errors

Finally I should add that the bulk of this book was written during the Christmas vacation. Although I tried not to let it intrude into the festivities too much, I apologise to my wife (Elizabeth) and daughter (Laura) if they sometimes thought my mind strayed back into the study even if my body remained firmly engrossed in Laura's new toys.

# Abbreviations

| | |
|---|---|
| CPA 1967 | Consumer Protection Act 1967 |
| DTI | Department of Trade and Industry |
| GPSR 1994 | General Product Safety Regulations 1994 |
| SGA 1979 | Sale of Goods Act 1979 |
| SG(A)A 1994 | Sale of Goods (Amendment) Act 1994 |
| SG(IT)A 1973 | Sale of Goods (Implied Terms) Act 1973 |
| SGSA 1982 | Supply of Goods and Services Act 1982 |
| SSGA 1994 | Sale and Supply of Goods Act 1994 |
| UCTA 1977 | Unfair Contract Terms Act 1977 |

# Table of Cases

# Table of Statutes

Page numbers in **bold** refer to quoted texts.

# Table of Statutory Instruments, Regulations and Directives

# 1

## Introduction

1994 was a significant year for the development of consumer sales legislation. Two statutes were passed amending the Sale of Goods Act 1979 — the Sale and Supply of Goods Act 1994 and the Sale of Goods (Amendment) Act 1994. The former also amended statutes governing contracts for the supply of goods otherwise than by sale. There were also two significant pieces of secondary legislation — the General Product Safety Regulations 1994 and the Unfair Terms in Consumer Contracts Regulations 1994. If these provisions had been enacted in one major consumer protection law they would no doubt have received wider publicity than they have achieved as individual pieces of reform. Yet their impact on the trading obligations of traders in consumer goods is no less significant due to the manner of their enactment.

### Sale and Supply of Goods Act 1994

The Sale and Supply of Goods Act 1994 essentially implements the Law Commission's proposals in its 1987 report, *Sale and Supply of Goods* (Law Com 160, Scot Law Com 104, Cm 137). This Act is broader than some of the other legislation covered in this book as it covers both consumer and commercial sales. Indeed the reform restricting the right of rejection where the breach is slight and it would be unreasonable to reject the goods only applies in non-consumer sales. The centrepiece of this Act is the replacement of the implied condition of merchantable quality with an implied term of satisfactory quality and the introduction of a list of factors which might be relevant when assessing quality. These provisions apply to sale contracts and also other contracts for the supply of goods covered by analogous legislation such as the Supply of Goods (Implied Terms) Act 1973 and the Supply of Goods and Services Act 1982.

Only the Sale of Goods Act 1979 has the concept of acceptance as a bar to rejection. This is reformed in the Sale and Supply of Goods Act 1994 by clarifying the relationship between the circumstances when acceptance is deemed to have occurred and the requirement that the buyer should have had a reasonable opportunity to examine the goods. A general right of partial rejection of goods is also introduced.

### Sale of Goods (Amendment) Act 1994

The Sale of Goods (Amendment) Act 1994 has abolished the market overt exception to the *nemo dat quod non habet* principle. This was a private member's Bill inspired by the belief that goods could be too easily sold at markets where, thanks to the market overt rule, the innocent purchaser could acquire a good title which defeated that of the original owner.

### Unfair Terms in Consumer Contracts Regulations 1994

The Unfair Terms in Consumer Contracts Regulations 1994 represent the United Kingdom's implementation of the EEC unfair terms in consumer contracts Directive. This introduces a general requirement that all terms which have not been individually negotiated in consumer contracts should be fair. Unfair terms are those which, contrary to the requirement of good faith, cause a significant imbalance in the parties' rights and obligations, to the detriment of the consumer. Individual consumers can seek to have unfair terms held to be non-binding, whilst the Director General of Fair Trading has new powers to seek injunctions against unfair terms.

### General Product Safety Regulations 1994

The General Product Safety Regulations 1994 implement the EEC general product safety Directive. They amend part II of the Consumer Protection Act 1987 to bring the general safety duty into line with the requirements of European law.

### Laws of European origin

Both the Unfair Terms in Consumer Contracts Regulations 1994 and the General Product Safety Regulations 1994 implement European Directives. This has the consequence that the laws must as far as possible be interpreted so as to comply with the Directives (see *Marleasing SA* v *La Comercial Internacional de Alimentación SA* (case C–106/89) [1990] ECR I-4135). This means not only should any obvious inconsistencies be remedied, but also application of the domestic law should take account of any interpretations (or potential interpretations) by the European Court of Justice regarding the meaning of the Directive. The General Product Safety Regulations came into force more than three months after the date set by the Directive and the Unfair Terms in Consumer Contracts Regulations will come into force six months late, on 1 July 1995. The position is unclear, but it is possible that member states may be liable in damages for loss suffered as a result of their failure to implement Directives on time (see *Francovich* v *Italian State* (Case C–6 & 9) [1991] ECR I-5357).

**An improvement?**

Most of the legislative reforms to consumer sales law in 1994 have undoubtedly improved the consumer's position. This has, however, been at the price of increasing the complexity of consumer law. The original Sale of Goods Act 1979 and part II of the Consumer Protection Act 1987 have been amended and the Unfair Terms in Consumer Contracts Regulations 1994 sit alongside common law and earlier statutory attempts to control unfair terms such as the Unfair Contract Terms Act 1977). Further reforms are suggested in other areas of consumer law and the time may soon be approaching when, even in the United Kingdom, the sense of a consolidated coherent consumer code is appreciated.

# 2

## Sale and Supply of Goods Act 1994

The Sale and Supply of Goods Act 1994 (hereafter SSGA 1994; see appendix 1) implements the proposals contained in the Law Commission report, *Sale and Supply of Goods* (Law Com 160, Scot Law Com 104, 1987, Cm 137). The main changes introduced are:

(a) The implied condition of merchantable quality is replaced by a term requiring goods to be of satisfactory quality.

(b) The rules in sale of goods contracts concerning when acceptance is deemed to have occurred and the relevance of the opportunity to examine the goods are reformulated.

(c) The buyer under a sales contract is given a right to accept part of a batch of goods which are defective whilst retaining the right to reject defective goods.

(d) The remedies for breach in non-consumer cases are modified so that rejection is not permitted where the breach is so slight that it would be unreasonable for the buyer to reject them.

### Application of the new law

The SSGA 1994 affects the law of the whole of the United Kingdom, that is, England and Wales, Northern Ireland and Scotland. This book will concentrate on explaining the effect of the changes in England and Wales. The effect of the changes in Northern Ireland and Scotland is similar except that in Scotland there are different rules on remedies for breach of contract and additionally sch. 1 to the SSGA 1994 amends the Supply of Goods and Services Act 1982 (hereafter SGSA 1982) so that the provisions of part I of that Act are extended to cover Scotland. Part I of the SGSA 1982 essentially extended the implied terms about title, description, quality and fitness and correspondence with sample to contracts involving the transfer of property in goods and hire contracts.

The Sale of Goods Act 1979 (hereafter SGA 1979) is the father of all legislation governing the supply of goods. The SSGA 1994 provides for amendments to be made to the SGA 1979. However, in recent times a number of other statutes have been passed to regulate contracts, other than sale contracts, which involve the supply of goods. Thus sch. 2 to the 1994 Act, in addition to making minor consequential amendments to the SGA 1979, also extends some of the reforms to other statutes. The other statutes include the Supply of Goods (Implied Terms) Act 1973 (hereafter SG(IT)A 1973), which regulates hire-purchase transactions; the SGSA 1982, which covers, *inter alia*, contracts for exchange or barter, work and materials, and hire; and the Trading Stamps Act 1964, which applies where trading stamps, e.g., Green Shield stamps, are used to obtain goods. The reforms which are extended to these analogous statutes are those relating to the satisfactory quality term and the restriction on the right to reject in non-consumer sales. The additional reforms concerning acceptance and the new rule that acceptance of some goods does not preclude the rejection of defective goods are irrelevant outside sale contracts as the SGA 1979 is the only Act which provides that acceptance bars rejection. Thus reference in this chapter will be to the SGA 1979 (indeed reference will usually be to the new provisions in the SGA 1979, rather than the sections in the SSGA 1994 which provided for the amendments), but the following table shows where equivalent provisions are to be found in the two other most significant Acts:

| *Sale of Goods Act 1979* | *Supply of Goods (Implied Terms) Act 1973* | *Supply of Goods and Services Act 1982* |
|---|---|---|
| s. 14 | s. 10 | ss. 4 and 9 |
| s. 15A | s. 11A | ss. 5A and 10A |

The most significant provisions of the SGA 1979, SG(IT)A 1973 and SGSA 1982 which have been amended by the SSGA 1994 are set out in their amended form in appendix 2.

The SSGA 1994 received the royal assent on 3 November 1994. Section 8(2) provides that it will come into force at the end of a period of two months beginning on the day it was passed. Therefore the new rules will apply to contracts entered into on or after 3 January 1995.

**Implied term as to quality**

*The old law — merchantable quality*

The common law had implied a term into sale contracts that goods would be of merchantable quality. When the common law was codified in the Sale of Goods Act 1893 the implied condition of merchantable quality was given statutory recognition. There were (and continue to be) also other implied conditions relating to the quality of goods, namely that the goods corresponded with their description, were fit for any particular purpose which the buyer had made known to the seller and that the goods corresponded with any sample. At that time these were default rules, which applied unless the parties specified otherwise, but in recent times the condition became non-excludable in consumer contracts and only excludable if reasonable in commercial contracts (see the Unfair Contract Terms Act 1977, ss. 6 and 7).

The content of the obligation to deliver goods of merchantable quality was rather obscure. There were two competing tests based around either the notion of 'usability' or 'acceptability'. Usability seemed more suited to commercial contracts whilst an acceptability standard, which was better able to take account of the non-functional aspects of the goods, seemed more suited to consumer transactions. In truth the courts never settled on one standard or the other and many judges applied tests which seemed to intermingle the two approaches. An example of the 'usability' approach was the statement of Lord Reid in *Henry Kendall and Sons* v *William Lillico and Sons Ltd* [1969] 2 AC 31 that 'unmerchantable' meant:

> that the goods in the form in which they were tendered were of no use for any purpose for which goods which complied with the description under which these goods were sold would normally be used, and hence were not saleable under that description.

An example of the 'acceptability' approach is provided by Dixon J of the High Court of Australia in *Australian Knitting Mills Ltd* v *Grant* (1933) 50 CLR 387, who said goods:

> should be in such an actual state that a buyer fully acquainted with the facts and, therefore, knowing what hidden defects exist and not being limited to their apparent condition would buy them without abatement of the price obtainable for such goods if in reasonably sound order and condition and without special terms.

The Law Commission had proposed a statutory definition based on the acceptability approach, but its definition was criticised as being too complicated and it eventually proposed a simpler standard based on the usability approach (*Exemption Clauses in Contracts First Report: Amendments to the Sale of Goods Act 1893* (Law Com 24, Scot Law Com 12), para. 43). This led to the enactment in the SG(IT)A 1973 of a provision which was consolidated in SGA 1979, s. 14(6). This provided that:

> Goods of any kind are of merchantable quality . . . if they are as fit for the purpose or purposes for which goods of that kind are commonly bought as it is reasonable to expect having regard to any description applied to them, the price (if relevant) and all the other relevant circumstances.

The emphasis on functionality caused the Law Commission in its 1987 report to criticise the condition as not being sufficiently consumer friendly. There was also criticism that 'merchantable quality' was an outdated term, and whilst its meaning might have been comprehensible to nineteenth-century merchants it sounded archaic in modern trading conditions, particularly in consumer transactions.

To some extent the judiciary had tried to meet these concerns and had attempted to give 'merchantable quality' a new consumer-friendly gloss. Thus in *Rogers v Parish (Scarborough) Ltd* [1987] QB 933, a case involving an expensive new Range Rover, Mustill LJ had said:

> the purpose for which 'goods of that kind' are commonly bought . . . would include in respect of any passenger vehicle not merely the buyer's purpose of driving the car from one place to another but of doing so with the appropriate degree of comfort, ease of handling and reliability and, one might add, of pride in the vehicle's outward and interior appearance.

Nevertheless the Law Commission favoured replacing 'merchantable quality' with a term requiring goods to be of acceptable quality and supporting this with a list of relevant factors. This is essentially the structure adopted in the SSGA 1994, save that the new term uses the word 'satisfactory' rather than acceptable quality. There appear to be two reasons for favouring satisfactory over acceptable as the adjective to define the quality level demanded. It is thought by some to be a more demanding standard as some consumers may accept goods they are not satisfied with. Also there was fear of some confusion if the word 'acceptable' was used, since acceptance is also the concept used to determine when the right to reject is lost.

In passing, it should be noted that there had been a previous attempt to implement the Law Commission's proposals in the Consumer Guarantees Bill 1990, but this had also tried to regulate consumer guarantees in a way which was unacceptable to the government and so had failed to be enacted. Also it should be noted that the other implied terms relating to fitness for a particular purpose, correspondence with description and correspondence with sample remain essentially unaltered.

*The new provision of satisfactory quality*

The SGA 1979, s. 14, now provides:

(2)   Where the seller sells goods in the course of a business, there is an implied term that the goods supplied under the contract are of satisfactory quality.

(2A)   For the purposes of this Act, goods are of satisfactory quality if they meet the standard that a reasonable person would regard as satisfactory, taking account of any description of the goods, the price (if relevant) and all the other relevant circumstances.

(2B)   For the purposes of this Act, the quality of goods includes their state and condition and the following (among others) are in appropriate cases aspects of the quality of goods—

(a)   fitness for all the purposes for which goods of the kind in question are commonly supplied,

(b)   appearance and finish,

(c)   freedom from minor defects,

(d)   safety, and

(e)   durability.

(2C)   The term implied by subsection (2) above does not extend to any matter making the quality of goods unsatisfactory—

(a)   which is specifically drawn to the buyer's attention before the contract is made,

(b)   where the buyer examines the goods before the contract is made, which that examination ought to reveal, or

(c)   in the case of a contract for sale by sample, which would have been apparent on a reasonable examination of the sample.

*In the course of a business*

Like its predecessor, merchantable quality, the satisfactory quality term is only implied into sale contracts made in the course of a business. The phrase 'in the course of a business', or similarly worded phrases, appears in other consumer protection statutes, notably the Trade Descriptions Act 1968 and the Unfair Contract Terms Act 1977. In both those contexts the phrase has been narrowly defined only to cover sales which formed an integral part of the seller's business (*Davies* v *Sumner* [1984] 1 WLR 1301 concerning a prosecution, under the Trade Descriptions Act 1968, of a self-employed courier who had falsely misrepresented the mileage when selling off his car) or buyer's business (*R & B Customs Brokers Co. Ltd* v *United Dominions Trust Ltd* [1988] 1 WLR 321, which concerned a company director who bought a car through the company but was nevertheless held to have bought a car when dealing as a consumer in order to benefit from the total ban on clauses excluding the implied quality conditions in consumer sales). A restricted interpretation of the phrase 'in the course of a business' might be appropriate in the context of trade descriptions law, so as not to impose criminal liability on private individuals, or under unfair contract terms legislation so as to extend the stricter protection afforded to consumers to small business people in certain circumstances. If a similar approach was taken in the present context then the law would be returned to the unsatisfactory position which existed prior to 1973 and which the SG(IT)A 1973 had sought to remedy. Prior to 1973 the merchantable quality condition had only been implied where the seller dealt in goods of that description. It is unlikely that in the context of implying quality conditions the phrase 'in the course of a business' would be given a restricted interpretation. This seems to have been underlined by Lord Wilberforce, who in *Ashington Piggeries Ltd* v *Christopher Hill Ltd* [1972] AC 441 said:

> I cannot comprehend the rationale of holding that the subsections do not apply if the seller is dealing in the particular goods for the first time. . . . what the Act had in mind was something quite simple and rational: to limit the implied conditions of fitness or quality to persons in the way of business, as distinct from private persons.

However, this may involve interpreting the phrase 'in the course of a business' differently in two different contexts under the same statute. This is because the SSGA 1994 introduces the phrase 'deals as a consumer' to differentiate between consumer and non-consumer sales for the purpose of restricting the remedies in non-consumer sales. 'Dealing as a consumer' is given the same definition as in the Unfair Contract Terms Act 1977: 'in the course of a business' forms a central part of that definition and, as already noted, in *R & B Custom Brokers Co. Ltd* v *United Dominions Trust Ltd* it was given a restricted interpretation in that context.

*Goods supplied*

The SGA 1979, s. 14(1), continues to state the basic principle that *caveat emptor* applies except as provided for by the implied terms of satisfactory quality, fitness for purpose and correspondence with sample. Section 14(1) states this principle applies to 'goods supplied under a contract of sale'. The phrase 'goods supplied' has been given a broad interpretation. It has been held to include (a) extraneous goods supplied with the goods contracted for (*Wilson* v *Rickett Cockerell & Co. Ltd* [1954] 1 QB 598, detonator included with Coalite!), and (b) packaging and containers supplied with the goods (*Geddling* v *Marsh* [1920] 1 KB 668, returnable mineral water bottle exploded).

*'Condition' and 'term'*

Whereas merchantable quality was labelled a 'condition', satisfactory quality is a 'term'. In fact the SSGA 1994, sch. 2, para. 5, provides that all the implied terms in the SGA 1979, ss. 12 to 15, are now labelled 'terms', rather than 'conditions' or 'warranties'. However, para. 5 also inserts new subsections, which in England and Wales categorise the terms as conditions or warranties, as before. For example, the new s. 14(6) now provides that the implied term about satisfactory quality is, in England and Wales and Northern Ireland, a condition. Classification of the term as a condition means that breach of the term gives rise to a right to reject.

*Reasonable person*

Goods are of satisfactory quality 'if they meet the standard that a reasonable person would regard as satisfactory'. The goods do not necessarily have to be perfect in every way and fit for every possible use. A reasonable person might, for instance, expect a second-hand car to have some minor scratches and would not expect the same performance from a family saloon as from a sports car. The term provides an open-textured standard giving the judge a wide discretion. This is necessary as the standard has to be applied to a wide range of goods. Ordinary consumer goods cover a wide range and the term also applies to industrial goods. It is also conceivable that the term applies to more esoteric goods such as blood and blood products and computer programs. The range of possible defects is as wide as the range of products. Defects may be unique to particular types of goods or even to individual items. The complaints can range from minor or cosmetic defects to complaints that the goods are not fit for the purpose, are dangerous or not sufficiently durable. These are the same problems which the courts were confronted with when judging whether goods were unmerchantable. A question, which is likely to be shortly before the courts, is whether previous case law can be relied upon. It may well be that satisfactory quality is a very similar standard to the more modern consumer-friendly approach to merchantable quality as epitomised by *Rogers* v *Parish (Scarborough) Ltd* [1987] QB 933, but it will be argued that there are dangers in seeking to rely on the old case law because satisfactory quality and merchantable quality are different standards.

*Relevance of the old law*

There was a rich case law surrounding merchantable quality. This was understandable when the content of the term was left undefined. Once a statutory definition had been provided, in 1973, one would have thought that it would have replaced the old case law. This was indeed the approach adopted by Mustill LJ in *Rogers* v *Parish (Scarborough) Ltd* [1987] QB 933 who considered that the definition being 'clear and free from technicality' should be capable of solving the majority of cases without reference to prior case law. However, by contrast, Lloyd LJ in *Aswan Engineering Establishment Co.* v *Lupdine Ltd* [1987] 1 WLR 1 took the view that the statutory definition was 'as accurate a representation of Lord Reid's speech in *Henry Kendall and Sons* v *William Lillico and Sons Ltd* [1969] 2 AC 31 as it is possible to compress into one sentence' and therefore felt free to rely on previous cases.

Even under the old regime Mustill LJ's approach might have been thought to be preferable. Given that any standard is always going to be a flexible one, leaving discretion in its application to the judge at first instance, there seems little point in confusing matters by unnecessarily importing technicalities from old case law. With the new standard of satisfactory quality, resorting to the old case law appears to be even more irrelevant, for two reasons. First, one of the justifications for referring to prior case law under the old regime, even after the enactment of a statutory definition, was because there was no guidance on what factors were relevant to the assessment of quality. The SSGA 1994, however, provides a non-exhaustive list of relevant factors. In so far as the old case law revolved around assessing the relevance of these factors, there would no longer appear to be any need to refer to jurisprudence on issues which have now been settled by statute. There may still be circumstances where old case law might be relied upon to show the relevance of a factor not expressly mentioned in the statute as being relevant, but no examples spring easily to mind. Second, another reason for looking at how previous cases were decided was to get an appreciation of how the standard had been previously applied against similar fact situations. Although it is unlikely that identical facts would be found in the case law, some guidance on how a court would treat a case could be gleaned from looking at the past application of the standard. However, now the goods are being judged against the standard of satisfactory quality rather than merchantable quality it does not make much sense to look at past decisions for this guidance. Even if the new satisfactory quality standard can be equated with merchantable quality as interpreted in recent pro-consumer cases like *Rogers v Parish (Scarborough) Ltd*, there is no guarantee that the standard will be identical. Indeed the fact that a conscious choice was made to adopt a standard of satisfactory, rather than acceptable quality as proposed by the Law Commission, suggests the reforms may be an attempt to raise standards. Furthermore, many of the old cases were decidedly less consumer friendly than *Rogers v Parish (Scarborough) Ltd* and so reference to them could be positively misleading. However, as the basic questions being asked are similar under both systems prior case law may be useful to illustrate the way in which various factors influence the assessment of the quality, even if the actual application differs in degree between the two schemes.

*Relevant factors*

The SSGA 1994 adopted the recommendation of the Law Commission and spelt out a list of relevant factors. These are:

(a)   fitness of all the purposes for which goods of the kind in question are commonly supplied,
(b)   appearance and finish,
(c)   freedom from minor defects,
(d)   safety, and
(e)   durability.

As will be seen, factors (b) to (e) make explicitly relevant factors which were probably implicit from the prior case law. This is, however, a welcome clarification, which at least pre-empts some possible legalistic arguments, which might otherwise have taken up the courts' time and the litigants' resources. Factor (a) is actually a revision of a factor which had previously formed part of the definition of merchantable quality. It is important to remember that the statute merely provides that these factors are in appropriate cases aspects of the quality of the goods. This does not mean that goods will automatically be of unsatisfactory quality just because one of these factors is present, for instance a minor defect. Rather, an overall assessment of the goods will have to be made, but it can no longer be denied that the factors listed above are relevant to the assessment of the goods' quality.

The SGA 1979 had also provided that '"quality" in relation to goods, includes their state or condition', but this was tucked away in s. 61(1) of the Act. It is more sensible for this statement to be included with the list of factors that are relevant when assessing quality. The SSGA 1994 has made this useful presentational amendment. The inclusion of state or condition means that, for instance, if goods have deteriorated or been damaged they may be of unsatisfactory quality even though they had at one time been satisfactory. Equally there is no need for a consumer to accept dirty goods on the basis that they will be fine when cleaned.

The definition of merchantable quality expressly stated that description and price were relevant factors. These factors are also expressly referred to in the definition of satisfactory quality: description must always be taken into account, but price is to be taken into account only if relevant.

The various factors will now be commented upon. Previous case law will be referred to amplify the points made, but the caveat must be added that the old cases considered these factors against the merchantable quality standard and the satisfactory quality standard may be more demanding. Equally in applying the test it must be remembered that every case will have unique facts and so past decisions can at best only be a guide (and now probably a fairly weak guide since a different standard was being applied).

*Description*

The description applied to goods can both raise and lower the standard of what a reasonable person would regard as satisfactory quality. Thus if goods are described as 'shop-soiled' or 'seconds' the reasonable person would expect the goods to be less than perfect. Equally the reasonable person would have lower expectations of goods described as 'second-hand' than would be appropriate for new goods. On the other hand the description 'antique' perhaps conjures up higher expectations in some contexts. Certainly descriptions such as 'luxury' or 'first-class' might raise the standard a reasonable person would be satisfied with. In *Rogers* v *Parish (Scarborough) Ltd* [1987] QB 933 Mustill LJ commented that '. . . the description "Range Rover" would conjure up a particular set of expectations'.

What forms part of the description of goods? Clearly it would cover anything stated orally by the seller or in writing, for example, an engineer's report sold with a second-hand car. It would also seem capable of covering the information provided on the packaging or containers supplied with the goods and might also cover information included in the advertising of the goods. It is perhaps unfortunate that the opportunity was not taken to make it clear that advertising and promotional material formed part of the description of the goods. It is also possible that the goods can describe themselves (in *Beale* v *Taylor* [1967] 1 WLR 1193 a badge saying '1200' on the back of the car led the buyer to believe that he was buying a 1961 Triumph Herald, when in fact it was two cars welded together).

As description forms part of the assessment of satisfactory quality, there is some degree of overlap with the SGA 1979, s. 13, which provides that goods must correspond with their description. The elements of the description which can form the basis of a claim under s.13 have been limited to those characteristics which are necessary to identify the goods and which are essential terms of the contract. The courts appear reluctant to allow other elements of the goods' description, to which the s. 13 door has been closed, to be brought in under the satisfactory quality term (see *Harlingdon and Leinster Enterprises Ltd* v *Christopher Hull Fine Art Ltd* [1990] QB 564, in which the contract concerned a sale of a painting between art dealers — the courts may be more lenient in the consumer context).

### Price

As a general rule the reasonable person expects higher-priced goods to be of superior quality to cheaper goods. Yet it is significant that the statute expressly states price should only be taken into account 'if relevant'. Certainly the mere fact that goods are reduced in price in a sale or promotion should not cause the reasonable person to expect them to be of lower quality than regularly priced goods. If there is some reason relating to their quality to explain why the goods are reduced, then their inferior quality should be signified through the use of words such as 'shop-soiled' rather than leaving the price to signify the lower quality.

A reasonable person, on finding low-priced goods, might consider that they were a bargain, rather than poor quality. Certainly even cheap goods should be fit for their basic purposes. A high price might tend to lead the reasonable person to expect, according to the nature of the goods concerned, (a) that the goods are of a higher-quality finish than usual; (b) that the model has features which are not on the standard model; or (c) where the goods are of a type which have different grades of quality, that the goods are of a high grade. It might also be suggested that people pay more for goods in the hope that the higher-priced goods will be more reliable. This is, however, a dangerous statement for the converse might be taken to mean that it is acceptable for lower-priced goods to be less reliable. A better way of putting this point is that all goods should function properly, but that in some cases it may be anticipated that higher-priced goods will continue to function properly for a longer period, i.e., be more durable. In general price should only be capable of raising not lowering the expectations a reasonable person has about the goods and this seems to be borne out by the case law on merchantable quality (*Rogers* v *Parish (Scarborough) Ltd* [1987] QB 933 in which it was held to be relevant that at £16,000 the Range Rover was well above the level of an ordinary family saloon; *Shine* v *General Guarantee Corporation Ltd* [1988] 1 All ER 911, in which the price reflected an enthusiast's car of that age, mileage and condition, rather than an insurance write-off).

*Fitness for all the purposes for which goods of the kind in question are commonly supplied*

As part of the definition of merchantable quality introduced in 1973 it was provided that goods had to be 'fit for the *purpose or purposes* for which goods of that kind are commonly bought' (emphasis added). The reference to purposes in the plural might have been taken to mean that goods had to be fit for more than one purpose, if the goods were capable of multiple uses. However, in *Aswan Engineering Establishment Co.* v *Lupdine Ltd* [1987] 1 WLR 1 it was held that goods had only to be fit for one purpose. The reference to purposes in the plural was said to have been included to cover goods of high quality, which might be expected to be fit for purposes over and above those expected from goods of the same type of lower quality. The new provision is significantly more demanding. It requires goods to be fit for '*all* the purposes for which goods of the kind in question are *commonly* supplied' (emphasis added). Goods must now be fit for all the common purposes not just one purpose. If goods are commonly supplied for a dozen purposes then the goods must be fit for each and every one of them. In theory, a court could still find goods which failed to perform one of the dozen purposes to be satisfactory, if it was not an appropriate case for regarding fitness for all common purposes as an aspect of quality. This would be highly unlikely, however. The court is more likely to avoid imposing liability by relying on the limiting factor that the goods must have been commonly supplied for that purpose. The court has a measure of discretion when determining what purposes goods were commonly supplied for. The requirement that the goods must have been commonly supplied for that purpose might mean that the decision in *Aswan Engineering Establishment Co.* v *Lupdine Ltd* would be the same under the new law. The facts of the case concerned plastic pails which melted when exposed to the Kuwaiti heat. If similar facts arose again it might be possible to argue that the plastic pails were not commonly supplied to be used in such heat and that a reasonable person would not expect them to capable of withstanding such temperatures. Of course, it remains possible for a seller to state expressly that the goods are suitable for only a limited range of purposes.

*Appearance and finish and freedom from minor defects*

The Law Commission preferred to separate out appearance and finish from minor defects. This is clearly a sensible approach. They relate to different types of defect — appearance and finish refer to cosmetic defects, whilst minor defects may be minor defects in the functioning of the goods, for example a cigarette lighter which does not work in a car. Many cosmetic defects relating to the appearance and finish of goods will be minor, but some can be so serious as to render the goods worthless: imagine a blouse with a large ink stain on it or a picture with a large rip in the canvas. However, the two factors have many common features and were often treated as being synonymous with each other under the old law and so they are conveniently discussed at the same time.

A good-quality appearance and finish of goods and freedom from minor defects are more likely to be expected by the reasonable person when buying luxury goods than when buying cheap mass-produced goods. It is therefore no coincidence that the modern case which recognised the significance of the appearance of goods concerned a £16,000 Range Rover. It will be remembered from the passage already quoted from Mustill LJ's judgment in *Rogers* v *Parish (Scarborough) Ltd* [1987] QB 933 that the purpose of driving a car was said to include 'doing so with the appropriate degree of comfort, ease of handling and reliability and . . . pride in the vehicle's outward and interior appearance'.

Whether the goods are new or second-hand will also be a relevant factor. Whilst one might expect new goods to be shining and perfect in every way, the reasonable person would anticipate that second-hand goods might show some signs of wear and tear and even that some non-essential parts might not function properly. For example, the interior light on a second-hand car might not work and there may be some scratches on the bodywork, but these defects need not necessarily render the goods unsatisfactory.

The mere fact that appearance and finish and freedom from minor defects are stated to be relevant to the issue of quality does not mean that any imperfection in these aspects will always render the goods unsatisfactory. The possibility of goods being held to be of satisfactory quality notwithstanding such defects has already been discussed in relation to second-hand goods, but could equally apply to new goods. Under the old law on merchantable quality a minor, cheap and easily repairable defect in a new car — for example, a leak in the power steering box, costing only £25 in 1973 prices to repair — was held not to have rendered a car unmerchantable: see *Millars of Falkirk Ltd* v *Turpie* (1976) SLT 66. It is entirely possible that the car would under the new law also be held to be of satisfactory quality, since a reasonable person would expect that some new cars had minor faults. However, it should continue to be the case that the possibility of repair under a manufacturer's guarantee should not be taken into account when assessing whether goods are of satisfactory quality, since guarantees should be viewed as additions to the legal minimum quality conditions: see *Rogers* v *Parish (Scarborough) Ltd* [1987] QB 933.

The fact that every cosmetic or minor defect does not automatically render the quality of the goods unsatisfactory does leave open the possibility that there may be no remedy at all under the implied quality conditions for some minor defects. The buyer would then be left to rely on any guarantee which had been supplied with the goods to get them repaired or replaced. This might suggest more attention be paid to the provision and regulation of guarantees, but although this lacuna is regrettable it may be better than providing a remedy short of rejection for minor defects. That approach would encourage defendants to argue that defects were minor to avoid the rejection remedy. In the commercial context this may be appropriate and later it will be shown that the SSGA 1994 does introduce a measure to cover this contingency in the commercial context. In the consumer context it would be a disaster because what consumers need to enforce laws effectively in practice are simple, straightforward, unambiguous rules and rights which they can assert. Introducing a grey area as to whether defects were major or minor would introduce the uncertainty for consumers which it had been sought to avoid by modifying remedies only in non-consumer cases.

*Safety*

Although no one could have doubted that goods would be unsatisfactory if they were unsafe, it is a useful clarification to have this spelt out for the avoidance of doubt. The rules on the quality of the goods therefore overlap with the product liability rules in part I of the Consumer Protection Act 1987. If an injured party can bring a claim in contract for breach of the implied term of satisfactory quality this may have the advantage that liability is strict and in particular the development risks defence is irrelevant to the contractual claim.

*Durability*

The relevance of durability to merchantable quality had been a moot point. The case law had dealt with durability in relation to the other implied term of fitness for particular purpose and had concentrated on how long goods had to be fit for (*Lambert* v *Lewis* [1982] AC 225 suggested goods had to be reasonably durable, but Lord Denning had doubted this in *Crowther* v *Shannon Motor Co.* [1975] 1 WLR 30). Durability is now clearly a factor which can be taken into account, but it must be remembered that goods only have to be durable for so long as a reasonable person would expect them to be. If goods prove not to be durable this will probably be taken as evidence that they were not of satisfactory quality at the time they were delivered, since presumably there must have been something wrong, even if it was not noticeable at the time of delivery, which caused the goods not to be reasonably durable.

The reluctance to admit the relevance of durability was in part explained by fears that it would lead to the buyer having a long-term right to reject the goods. In sale contracts this fear is unfounded as rejection of the goods is precluded by acceptance, which is deemed to take place after the goods have been retained for a reasonable period of time. In other supply contracts rejection is only prevented once the buyer is aware of the defect and has affirmed the contract. Thus in hire-purchase, exchange or barter, or contracts for work and materials the inclusion of durability will give rise to the long-term right to reject. However, in cases involving an element of hire justice will be achieved by allowing the seller an allowance for the use of the goods (see *Charterhouse Credit Co. Ltd* v *Tolley* [1963] 2 QB 683; cf. *Farnworth Finance Facilities Ltd* v *Attryde* [1970] 1 WLR 1053 where it was said that the value of any use was offset by the great amount of trouble the buyer experienced). In other supply contracts the courts will probably have to rethink the rules on restitution of the price based on a total failure of consideration. Generally enjoyment of the subject-matter should not bar a claim on the basis of a total failure of consideration, but such a rule if extended to cases of lack of durability could be a source of injustice.

During the passage of the Bill which was enacted as the SSGA 1994 there were attempts to amend it to include provisions on spare parts and after-sales service. These were, however, resisted and such matters continue only to be controlled by codes of practice.

*Knowledge*

If the buyer knew or ought to have known of the lack of satisfactory quality then the satisfactory quality term cannot be invoked by the buyer. Similar rules applied in relation to merchantable quality.

The satisfactory quality term does not extend to any matter making the goods unsatisfactory which is specifically drawn to the buyer's attention before the contract is made or, where the buyer examines the goods before the contract is made, which that examination ought to reveal. This is similar to the old wording, but may be slightly more generous to the seller. Under merchantable quality the *defect* had to be drawn to the buyer's attention or revealed by the examination. Under satisfactory quality it is sufficient that a matter making the goods unsatisfactory be drawn to the buyer's attention or revealed by the examination. It may be that the matter is not the defect itself, but something which renders the goods defective. However, this may be playing with semantics and the new rules can be seen as essentially the same as the old. It is important to remember that there is no obligation on a buyer to examine the goods and the buyer is only unable to rely on the satisfactory quality term as regards matters which the examination actually made ought to have revealed. Thus if a buyer makes an examination of the exterior of the car, the examination would not reveal faults with the engine and so the buyer could still invoke the satisfactory quality term to complain about mechanical defects.

In the case of a contract for sale by sample the satisfactory quality term does not extend to any matter making the quality of goods unsatisfactory which would have been apparent on a reasonable examination of the sample. This contrasts with normal sale contracts, where the buyer is only presumed to know of matters which ought to have been revealed by an examination which had actually been made: in the case of sale by sample there may be constructive knowledge. Thus, if the matter would have been apparent had a reasonable examination of the sample been undertaken then the buyer cannot claim to be unaffected by knowledge of the matter because of not carrying out any examination.

### Remedies for breach of condition

*Rejection, damages, repair, replacement and the right to cure*

The implied term of satisfactory quality is a condition (SGA 1979, s. 14(6)). Breach of condition, like breach of warranty, gives rise to a claim for damages. Additionally, however, breach of condition allows the buyer to reject the goods, a remedy which is not available for mere breach of warranty. In most cases rejection of the goods will also repudiate the contract. However, a buyer could reject goods, but invite the seller to retender goods of satisfactory quality. It is even sometimes suggested that the seller should be able to retender goods if the contract date for delivery has not passed; but the cases supporting this have involved the tender of defective documents and it may be simpler to amend documents than to cure goods (*Borrowman Phillips and Co.* v *Free and Hollis* (1878) 4 QBD 500). Certainly in the consumer context the buyer should be able to rely on his loss of confidence in the seller to justify refusing an attempt to cure. Apart from this limited right of the seller to affect a cure, it is an irony that the buyer has no right to claim repair or replacement of unsatisfactory goods, despite these being the two remedies which consumers most frequently invoke. The right of rejection is a powerful weapon in the armoury of the dissatisfied buyer. The only problem with the right of rejection is that it is too easily lost.

*Acceptance*

The SGA 1979, s. 11(4), provides that:

> Subject to section 35A below where a contract of sale is not severable, and the buyer has accepted the goods or part of them, the breach of a condition to be fulfilled by the seller can only be treated as a breach of warranty, and not as a ground for rejecting the goods and treating the contract as repudiated, unless there is an express or implied term of the contract to that effect.

Previously s. 35 of the SGA 1979 had set out three circumstances when the buyer was deemed to have accepted the goods, namely, by intimation of acceptance, by the doing of an act inconsistent with the seller's ownership and by retaining the goods for a reasonable period of time without intimating rejection (as these circumstances remain the same it is not proposed to go into detail on their meaning and interpretation: the reader is referred to standard works on the subject, for instance, Benjamin's *Sale of Goods,* 4th ed. (London: Sweet & Maxwell, 1992), paras 12-049–12-064).

*Intimation of acceptance and act inconsistent with the seller's ownership*

The SGA 1979, s. 34(1), provided that a buyer who has not previously examined the goods will not be deemed to have accepted them until there has been a reasonable opportunity of examining them to ascertain if they are in conformity with the contract. The relationship between ss. 34 and 35 was obscure. Section 34 was stated to apply to the second instance of deemed acceptance, namely, the doing of any act inconsistent with the seller's ownership. It seemed that an opportunity for examination was not a requirement for there to be deemed acceptance on the basis of an intimation of acceptance. Although the position was unclear in relation to deemed acceptance by the retention of goods, where goods had been retained for a reasonable period of time the buyer would usually have had a reasonable opportunity to examine them. The Law Commission recommended reform of the rules on acceptance, including the relationship between s. 34 and s. 35. These recommendations resulted in the SSGA 1994 repealing s. 34(1) and amending s. 35(1) of the SGA 1979. Section 34(1) is repealed by SSGA 1994, s. 2(2)(a) but the provision which was formally s. 34(2) is retained. This provides that, unless otherwise agreed, when the seller tenders delivery of the goods, he is bound on request to afford the buyer a reasonable opportunity of examining the goods for the purpose of ascertaining whether they are in conformity with the contract (s. 34). Additionally, since the SSGA 1994 the reasonable opportunity to examine extends in the cases of a contract for sale by sample to comparing the bulk with the samples.

The SGA 1979, s. 35 as amended by the SSGA 1994, s. 2(1), continues to provide that there will be acceptance (a) when the buyer intimates to the seller that the goods have been accepted and (b) when the goods have been delivered and the buyer does any act in relation to them which is inconsistent with the ownership of the seller (s. 35(1)). It is now, however, made clear that where the goods are delivered to a buyer who has not previously examined them, there will be no acceptance until the buyer has had a reasonable opportunity of examining them for the purpose of ascertaining whether they are in conformity with the contract and, in the case of a contract for sale by sample, of comparing the bulk with the sample (s. 35(2)).

Previously, s. 15(2)(b) provided that in contracts for sale by sample there was an implied condition that the buyer would have a reasonable opportunity of comparing the bulk with the sample. This provision is now repealed, but the position is likely to be the same under the new rules that on request the seller should afford the buyer a reasonable opportunity of examining the goods in a case of a contract for sale by sample to compare the bulk with the sample (s. 34) and that there is no acceptance by virtue of intimation of acceptance or the doing of an act inconsistent with the seller's ownership until there has been a reasonable opportunity for examination.

A buyer who deals as consumer (the meaning of this phrase is explained at page 26) cannot, by agreement, waiver or otherwise, lose the right to have a reasonable opportunity to examine the goods before acceptance is deemed (s. 35(3)). This implies, however, that where the buyer does not deal as a consumer, e.g., in a business transaction, the parties can agree to waive the right to examine the goods.

*Lapse of a reasonable period of time*

The third situation where acceptance is deemed to have occurred is when the buyer, after the lapse of a reasonable time, retains the goods without intimating to the seller that they have been rejected (SGA 1979, s. 35(4)). In determining whether a reasonable time has elapsed it will be a material question whether the buyer has had a reasonable opportunity of examining the goods (s. 35(5)). This would seem to bar rejection where the goods lack durability, for by the time the weakness became apparent there would presumably have been a reasonable opportunity to examine the goods, even though the examination would not, perhaps, have revealed the defect.

Consideration of the opportunity to examine the goods might assist buyers in circumstances where previously they would have lost the right to reject. For instance, in *Bernstein* v *Pamson Motors (Golders Green) Ltd* [1987] 2 All ER 220, the plaintiff was held to have lost the right to reject a new car when three weeks had elapsed during which the buyer had been ill and had only driven the car for 142 miles. Rougier J noted that the right to reject was lost after the lapse of a reasonable period of time and there was no qualification that the time should be sufficient to provide an opportunity to discover the defect. This point has been corrected by the amendments made by the SSGA 1994, although the case still shows that what is considered a reasonable time will depend upon the particular facts of individual cases.

During the course of the Parliamentary debates, the example was given of a consumer fitting a kitchen. An oven was purchased, but due to a delay in the units being delivered it remained (sensibly to prevent damage) unpacked and unexamined for three months. Had the right to reject been lost? A reasonable period of time might have elapsed, but had there been a reasonable opportunity to examine the goods? Whilst there had been plenty of opportunities to examine the goods, it is at least arguable that none of these were reasonable since it would have been unreasonable to expect the consumer to unpack the goods before they could be installed. The question remains an open one, but the new provision at least offers the possibility of the courts arriving at sensible conclusions based on the facts of individual cases.

*Repair*

It was sometimes suggested that agreement by a buyer to an attempt to repair goods could preclude the buyer from rejecting the goods, even if the repair was unsuccessful. This was because agreeing to have the goods repaired could be taken as intimating acceptance of them or as an act inconsistent with the seller's ownership. It is now provided that the buyer is not deemed to have accepted the goods merely because of having asked for, or agreed to, their repair by or under an arrangement with the seller (s. 35(6)(a)). The section does not preclude, in appropriate cases, an agreement to repair amounting to acceptance, but such instances are likely to be rare and certainly the mere fact of repair cannot be relied on alone as evidence of acceptance. The section, however, only covers repairs by or under an arrangement with the seller. If a buyer took the goods to an independent third party for repair this would more than likely be treated as amounting to acceptance of the goods, unless perhaps the repair was effected in an emergency.

The Law Commission, in its 1987 report, considered that if this reform was implemented then the courts would also not count time during which the goods were in for repair when determining whether the goods were deemed to have been accepted because a reasonable period of time had elapsed without an intimation of rejection. This obviously seems a sensible approach and it is perhaps unfortunate that this was not stated explicitly in the statute.

In some legal systems where repair is a remedy provided for defective goods it is also provided that the buyer retains the right to reject the goods if the repair is unsuccessful. Such a provision should be unnecessary under English law, since the effect of this reform is that most buyers will not lose the right to reject goods by merely agreeing to an attempt to repair them. In the rare cases where acceptance can be found from the buyer's act of having them repaired damages will be the only remedy.

*Subsales*

The Law Commission was unhappy with the phrase 'an act . . . inconsistent with the ownership of the seller'. There were two strands of cases where acceptance was deemed on this basis. One concerned instances where the buyer was unable to return the goods or it would be unreasonable for them to be returned. This might be because the goods had been destroyed, damaged or incorporated into other property or because the goods had been used for longer than was necessary to test them. Another group of cases found acceptance by virtue of the buyer having made a subsale of the goods. Often the buyer would subsell goods and arrange for them to be delivered direct to the third party. If they were defective the third party would reject them, but the original buyer would be unable to reject them as the act of subsale would be deemed to be an acceptance. This problem should be overcome by the new requirement in SGA 1979, s. 35(2), that the buyer be given a reasonable opportunity to examine the goods before acceptance is deemed on the basis of an act inconsistent with the seller's ownership, However, subsales normally occur in non-consumer cases, where the contract can waive the right to a reasonable opportunity to examine the goods. To avoid doubt it is provided that the buyer is not deemed to have accepted the goods merely because the goods are delivered to another under a subsale or other disposition (s. 35(6)(b)). Note the section does not say a subsale cannot be deemed an acceptance, merely that on its own without further evidence it need not be treated as an acceptance.

### Commercial unit

Where the contract is for the sale of goods making up one or more commercial units, a buyer accepting any goods included in a unit is deemed to have accepted all the goods making the unit. 'Commercial unit' means a unit, which if divided would materially impair its value or character (s. 35(7)).

### Right of partial rejection

The SGA 1979, s. 11(4), deprives the buyer of the right to reject after having accepted the goods or part of them. Thus in principle there is no right of partial rejection. Section 30(4) had provided an exception to this where goods of the contract description had been supplied mixed with goods of a different description. The buyer had the right to accept only the goods which were in accordance with the contract description or reject the whole. This has now been repealed by SSGA 1994, s. 3(3), but in line with the Law Commission's recommendations a new broader right of partial rejection has been introduced in the new s. 35A of the SGA 1979.

Section 35A provides that if the buyer has the right to reject goods by reason of a breach on the part of the seller that affects some or all of the goods, then by accepting some of them the buyer does not lose the right to reject the rest. However, where there are any goods unaffected by the breach the buyer must have accepted all such goods. Therefore where all the goods are affected by the breach the buyer can choose how many to accept. However, if there are some non-defective goods then partial acceptance of the defective ones is allowed only if all the non-defective goods are accepted: otherwise everything must be rejected.

Goods are deemed to be affected by a breach if they are not in conformity with the contract. Conformity with the contract is left undefined, but can probably be understood to mean conformity with any express contractual terms and the implied terms (e.g., those relating to title, correspondence with description, satisfactory quality, fitness for particular purpose and correspondence with sample).

The right of partial rejection can be excluded or modified by a contrary intention which appears in, or can be implied from, the contract.

The rules on acceptance and partial rejection apply only to sale of goods contracts. This is because the other analogous supply contracts do not contain rules restricting the right to reject by the concept of acceptance. Instead they require the buyer to have knowledge of the breach and to affirm the contract or waive the breach.

*Modification of breach of condition in non-consumer cases*

The right to reject is a powerful weapon. It applies to breach of any condition, including those implied by the SGA 1979 and the statutes covering other contracts for the supply of goods. As liability for breach of condition is strict, and the remedy of rejection arises no matter how minor the breach, there is the possibility of abuse. Although minor defects might not be sufficient to breach the satisfactory quality condition, they might breach other conditions such as the requirement that goods comply with their description. There have been notorious examples of breach of condition being used as an excuse for rejecting goods and repudiating the contract. For instance, *Re Moore and Co. and Landauer and Co. Ltd* [1921] 2 KB 519 concerned an order for 3,000 tins of canned fruit. The correct number of tins was delivered, but half of the cases contained 24 instead of the specified 30 tins. Rejection was allowed despite an arbitrator's finding that the value of the goods was unaffected. Such reported instances of rejection for minor defects have tended to occur in the commercial context, where the reason for rejection is normally factors external to the contract itself, such as the buyer wishing to reject goods ordered so as to benefit from falling prices. Such external factors are less likely to influence consumers and there is little evidence that consumers seek to reject goods on unreasonable grounds. Indeed there are strong arguments to support the retention for consumers of the clear and automatic right to reject non-conforming goods. Consumers do not have the legal expertise to decide if a breach is sufficiently serious to justify rejection and because of their weak bargaining position may feel forced to accept the seller's offer of repair.

The Law Commission distinguished between consumer and non-consumer sales. It thought that only in non-consumer sales should the right to reject be modified. However, it rejected the common law test set out in *Hongkong Fir Shipping Co. Ltd* v *Kawasaki Kisen Kaisha Ltd* [1962] 2 QB 26, which, for innominate terms, allowed rejection only when the breach was so serious as to frustrate the contract. Instead the Commission wanted simply to remove abuses by preventing rejection where the breach was so slight that it would be unreasonable for the buyer to reject. This is implemented by the SSGA 1994 inserting a new s. 15A into the SGA 1979 and equivalent provisions into the SG(IT)A 1973 and the SGSA 1982.

The SGA 1979, s. 15A, applies where, in a contract of sale, the buyer would otherwise have the right to reject goods by reason of a breach by the seller of s. 13 (correspondence with description), s. 14 (satisfactory quality and fitness for purpose) or s. 15 (correspondence with sample). It provides that if the breach is so slight that it would be unreasonable for the buyer to reject the goods then the breach is not to be treated as a breach of condition, but may be treated as a breach of warranty. Thus the possibility of rejection is removed and the buyer is restricted to a claim in damages under the warranty. The use of the word 'may' is rather strange: 'shall' would have been a more appropriate verb to use, for there seems to be no alternative way of dealing with the breach.

The restrictions on the right to reject apply only where the buyer does not deal as consumer. The phrase 'deal as consumer' is borrowed from the Unfair Contract Terms Act 1977 (hereafter UCTA 1977). SGA 1979, s. 61(5A), provides that 'dealing as consumer' shall have the same definition as is provided for in part I of UCTA 1977 where s. 12 states that a party to a contract 'deals as consumer' if:

(a)   he neither makes the contract in the course of a business nor purports to do so; and

(b)   the other party does make the contract in the course of a business; and

(c)   in the case of a sale of goods or hire-purchase contract the goods are of a type ordinarily supplied for private use or consumption.

In a sale by auction or competitive tender the buyer is never regarded as dealing as consumer. The case of *R & B Custom Brokers Co. Ltd* v *United Dominions Trust Ltd* [1988] 1 WLR 321 has already been discussed. That case gave a limited interpretation of 'in the course of a business' so that a company director buying a car through the company was nevertheless considered to be dealing as consumer.

The SGA 1979, s. 15A, applies only where the buyer does not deal as consumer. The burden is on the seller to prove both (a) that the buyer does not deal as consumer (s. 61(5A)), and (b) that the breach is so slight that it would be unreasonable for the buyer to reject the goods (s. 15A(3)). The parties are free to agree that the restrictions on the right to reject should not apply. Such a contrary intention may appear in, or be implied from, the contract.

*Delivery of a shortfall or excess*

The SGA 1979, s. 30(1), gave the buyer the right to reject goods if the seller delivered a quantity less than that contracted for. Where a larger quantity than contracted for was delivered, s. 30(2) allowed the buyer to accept the goods included in the contract and reject the rest, or reject the whole. The SSGA 1994 restricts these rights of rejection. Section 30(2D) restricts the right to reject under s. 30(1) and (2) to cases where the shortfall or excess is material. The new s. 30(2A) of the SGA 1979 provides that in these circumstances a buyer who does not deal as consumer may not reject the whole of the goods if the shortfall, or excess, is so slight that rejection would be unreasonable. Again the burden is on the seller to show (a) that the buyer did not deal as consumer (s. 61(5A)) and (b) to show that the shortfall or excess was so slight as to make rejection unreasonable (s. 30(2B)).

## The future

There have long been calls for an overhaul of sales legislation. These latest reforms might be viewed as sticking plaster on legislation which is in need of a more fundamental reappraisal. This criticism can be levelled even more forcefully at the very partial reform of the *nemo dat quod non habet* principle attempted by the Sale of Goods (Amendment) Act 1994, which is considered in the next chapter. Indeed a case can be made out for separate rules to govern commercial and consumer transactions, although there will inevitably be difficult questions as to where to draw the line between the two systems.

   More immediately United Kingdom sales law is likely to be affected by European law. Article 6 of the second draft Directive on unfair contract terms (OJ C 73/7, 24.3.92) had proposed rules governing the minimum quality of goods. These were removed from the final version of the Directive and the Commission was asked to look at the issue in depth. The result was the Green Paper on *Guarantees for Consumer Goods and After-sales Services* (COM (93) 509). Note that the proposals relate only to consumer goods. Any Directive which emerges is likely to be of a minimum character allowing member States to retain more protective laws. This may be an important safeguard for United Kingdom consumers if the Continental tradition of permitting the seller to attempt cure is adopted. The actual minimum quality standard mandated is unlikely to be more demanding than the implied quality conditions contained in the SGA 1979 and analogous legislation. However, it is possible that a Directive would require the rules on privity to be relaxed. This may involve allowing consumers to sue manufacturers or allowing persons other than the original purchaser, for example, donees of a gift or subsequent purchasers to rely on the rights under the sale contract. The Green Paper also covers the topic of commercial guarantees, e.g., the guarantees voluntarily given by manufacturers, and after-sales service. These proposals may take some time to come to fruition, but when they do they may provide the excuse for the creation of distinct schemes to govern commercial and consumer transactions.

# 3

## Sale of Goods (Amendment) Act 1994

Like the Sale and Supply of Goods Act 1994, the Sale of Goods (Amendment) Act 1994 (hereafter SG(A)A 1994; see appendix 3) received royal assent on 3 November 1994 and, also like the former Act, came into force two months later, i.e., 3 January 1995. The SG(A)A 1994 applies to any contract for the sale of goods made after that date. The purpose of the Act is simple: to abolish the rule of market overt. This rule potentially enabled stolen goods to be disposed of at certain markets in a way which gave the buyer a title which defeated the claim of the person from whom the goods were stolen. The motivation for the reform was the belief that the provision allowed markets to be used as a place for stolen goods to be sold in a way which defeated the claim of the true owners. This reform, perhaps, misunderstood the limited nature of the market overt rule and certainly showed a contrary policy to most of the recent reform proposals in this area. These points will be amplified, but first the market overt rule will be placed in the context of general rules on the transfer of title.

### Nemo dat quod non habet

A basic principle of English sales law is expressed in the Latin maxim *nemo dat quod non habet*: one cannot give what one does not have, a purchaser of goods cannot acquire any better title to them than the seller had. This is given statutory recognition in the SGA 1979, s. 21(1). This reflects the law's interest in protecting property rights, but the law of sale also seeks to promote commercial activity and this might be stunted if buyers could not be confident of acquiring good title in the goods they purchased. As Denning LJ said, in an oft-quoted dictum, in *Bishopsgate Motor Finance Corporation Ltd* v *Transport Brakes Ltd* [1949] 1 KB 322:

In the development of our law, two principles have striven for mastery. The first is for the protection of property: no one can give a better title than he himself possesses. The second is for the protection of commercial transactions: the person who takes in good faith and for value without notice should get a good title.

## Exceptions

The SGA 1979 itself provides for exceptions to the *nemo dat* principle where the owner is estopped from denying the seller's title or the seller is the owner's agent (s. 21(1)). The agency principles are given an extended ambit by the express preservation, in s. 21(2)(a), of the power of mercantile agents to pass title under the Factors Acts (defined in s. 61(1) to mean the Factors Act 1889, the Factors (Scotland) Act 1890, and any enactment amending or substituted for those Acts). Section 21(2)(b) preserves the validity of sale contracts under common law or statutory powers or under a court order. Special provisions apply allowing, in appropriate circumstances, a good title to pass where a sale is made by a seller of goods with a voidable title (s. 23), by a seller in possession after a sale (s. 24) and by a buyer in possession after a sale (s. 25). The SGA 1979 is the only statute governing the supply of goods to have a comprehensive regime governing the transfer of title. But as it was a codification of common law principles it can be assumed that similar rules apply to other contracts for the supply of goods, adapted of course to the nature of the legal interest which is being transferred. Part III of the Hire-Purchase Act 1964 does, however, provide a scheme whereby private purchasers acting in good faith can obtain a good title to motor vehicles despite their being subject to hire-purchase or conditional sale agreements.

## Market overt

The above-mentioned exceptions to the *nemo dat* principle tend to help a third party who buys goods from someone who exceeded the authority of the true owner or duped the true owner. They are of little assistance where the goods have been stolen. The market overt exception did allow an innocent purchaser to acquire good title in stolen goods. The SGA 1979, s. 22(1), provided:

Where goods are sold in market overt, according to the usage of the market, the buyer acquires a good title to the goods, provided he buys them in good faith and without notice of any defect or want of title on the part of the seller.

This provision is repealed by the SG(A)A 1994, s. 1.

Not all sales in markets were covered by the section. The market had to be a market overt. This covered every shop within the boundaries of the City of London. But in the rest of London and elsewhere in England markets overt were restricted to open, public, legally constituted markets and fairs. To be legally constituted the market or fair must either have been created by statute or charter or be established by long continual user. Thus the majority of car boot sales taking place on public house car parks or school premises would not be covered by the market overt exception to the *nemo dat* principle. The market overt rule had been abolished for Wales as far back as 1542, by the Laws in Wales Act 1542, s. 47, which is repealed and superseded by the SG(A)A 1994.

Not all sales in market overt were covered. The buyer must have bought the goods in good faith and without notice of any defect or want of title on the part of the seller. The goods must be sold 'according to the usage of the market'. Thus in relation to the sale of goods in a shop in the City of London it has been held that the sale must have taken place in the ordinary part of the shop, not, for instance, in a back room. In markets and fairs the goods must have been exposed for sale in the normal way. The sale must have been made on a normal market day and during normal hours (in one case the rule was said not to apply to a sale made during the half-light before dawn: *Reid* v *Metropolitan Police Commissioner* [1973] QB 551). The goods must have been of a description ordinarily sold at that market and sales to traders were not covered. All this seems to be in keeping with one of the explanations for the rule: that in former times, when goods were not so easily transported, a person who had goods stolen from him could be expected to search the markets for them and if he failed to discover them it would be unfair to allow him to reclaim them from an innocent purchaser, who bought them at a public market. This was perhaps never very fair, but of course is less so nowadays when thieves can easily dispose of goods at the other end of the country. This, combined with the fears of a thief's paradise created by the explosion of car boot sales, explains why abolishing the rule was seen as desirable. An alternative justification for the rule was that it promoted the confidence of persons to buy in market overt. Ironically, at the same time as the market overt rule was abolished, the trend in reform proposals in this area has been towards certainty in commercial transactions by favouring the innocent purchaser.

## Reform

The Law Reform Committee's *Twelfth Report: Transfer of Title to Chattels* (1966) had also proposed abolishing the market overt rule, but went on to suggest replacing it with a provision enabling a person who buys goods in good faith by retail at trade premises or at a public auction to acquire a good title. This report has been left to gather dust. In 1989 Professor Diamond issued a report, *A Review of Security Interests in Property*, in which he proposed a general principle to the effect that wherever the owner of goods has entrusted them to, or acquiesced in their possession by, another person, a disposition by the possessor in favour of an innocent party would confer good title on the purchaser, to the extent that the owner could have conferred title. In January 1994 the Department of Trade and Industry issued a consultation paper, *Transfer of Title: Sections 21 to 26 of the Sale of Goods Act 1979*, which broadly favoured reform along the lines proposed by Professor Diamond. The idea of this reform is to favour innocent purchasers, not where goods have been stolen, but rather where the owners have been instrumental in the seller having possession of the goods. This is less radical than the original reform proposals of the Law Reform Committee and in his submissions to that committee Professor Diamond had himself favoured a more extreme rule, under which any innocent purchaser of goods who had acted reasonably should be able to retain the goods. It is clear from this brief survey of proposals for reform that abolition of the market overt rule by itself is only a partial solution to the problems which are encountered in this area of the law.

# 4

# Unfair Terms in Consumer Contracts Regulations 1994

The Unfair Terms in Consumer Contracts Regulations 1994 (SI 1994/3195; see appendix 4) implement the EEC Directive on unfair terms in consumer contracts (93/13/EEC, OJ L 95/29, 21.4.93; see appendix 5). The Directive was required to be implemented by 31 December 1994. The Regulations were made on 8 December 1994, laid before Parliament on 14 December 1994 and will come into force on 1 July 1995 (reg. 1). This is six months after the date set for implementation by the Directive and therefore potentially exposes the United Kingdom government to an action under the *Francovich* principle, if someone suffers damages as a result of the inclusion in a contract of a term which would have been non-binding had the Directive been implemented on time (see page 3).

It might have been considered unfair on industry to make it comply with Regulations just two or three weeks after they were made and before they were available from HMSO. On the other hand, it could be argued that industry should have been aware of the basic thrust of the laws since the Directive was adopted in April 1993 and certainly since the consultation process started by the DTI. In fact the DTI first published a consultation document on this topic in October 1993, entitled *Implementation of the EC Directive on Unfair Terms in Consumer Contracts*, and a further consultation document with the same title in September 1994 (hereafter respectively, Consultation Document and Further Consultation Document). The decision to postpone the coming into force is, however, better than the solution proposed in the Further Consultation Document. This had suggested that the Regulations should come into force at the latest by 31 December 1994, but that terms in standard-form contracts would not be assessed for fairness if identical terms had been offered to consumers generally by the seller or supplier at any time during the six months prior to the Regulations coming into force. Leaving aside the many technical questions of interpretation this provision would have given rise to, it would also have generated unfairness by penalising those sellers and suppliers who attempted to update their terms before 1 July 1995. At least the new date for the coming into force of the Regulations clearly applies equally to all contracts, even if it does technically breach the United Kingdom's European obligations.

### A new layer

The Directive imposed a time limit of less than two years for implementation. This is relatively short, but in fact as member States had been aware of the possibility of such reform since at least the publication of the first draft Directive on the subject in 1990, it was not an unreasonable period. However, given the time-consuming nature of legislative procedure and the pressure for space in the Parliamentary calendar it was considered desirable to implement the Directive by means of secondary legislation under s. 2(2) of the European Communities Act 1972. The time-scale for implementation no doubt also partly explained why the Regulations were not integrated into the existing statutory scheme, namely the Unfair Contract Terms Act 1977 (hereafter UCTA 1977). The DTI has suggested that the concepts of reasonableness under the UCTA 1977 and unfairness under the Directive may be similar but are not the same. The DTI may well therefore be right to state that the Directive could not have been implemented using the reasonableness standard, but consideration could have been given to adopting the Directive's fairness standard as part of an integrated reform which consolidated the current reforms into the structure of the UCTA 1977 (see Further Consultation Document, p. 3). Instead there are now three layers of regulation of unfair terms in consumer contracts:

(a)   the common law, which applies to all contracts regardless of whether one party is a consumer, although the position of the consumer may be relevant to the application of some of the rules;

(b)   the UCTA 1977 which applies to all contracts, but has specially protective provisions for consumer contracts;

(c)   the Regulations, which only apply to consumer contracts and indeed only to terms which have not been individually negotiated.

The common law and the UCTA 1977 will be briefly described before the new Regulations are considered in detail.

*Common law*

The common law had some substantive controls over unfair terms, notably those relating to relief from forfeiture and penalty clauses. The majority of common law rules, however, were concerned with procedural rules such as the principles of mistake, misrepresentation, undue influence, economic duress and unconscionability. Although these rules were not created specifically to protect consumers, they have been used to assist consumers as many of them take account of the weak bargaining position a consumer is often in.

*Unfair Contract Terms Act 1977*

Although other statutes do regulate unfair terms (see, for instance, the extortionate credit bargain provisions in the Consumer Credit Act 1974, ss. 137 to 140), the UCTA 1977 is the most important statute regulating unfair terms in the United Kingdom. The Act applies differently to consumer and non-consumer contracts. The most important provisions regulating unfair terms in consumer contracts are those:

　(a)　preventing the exclusion or restriction of liability for death or personal injury resulting from negligence;

　(b)　subjecting exclusions or restrictions of liability for other losses resulting from negligence to a reasonableness test;

　(c)　preventing unreasonable restrictions or limitations on liability resulting from breach of contract;

　(d)　preventing unreasonable claims to be entitled to render a contractual performance substantially different from that which was reasonably expected or to render no performance at all in respect of the whole or part of a party's contractual obligations;

　(e)　preventing consumers from being subjected to unreasonable indemnity clauses;

　(f)　preventing guarantees from being used to restrict liability in negligence for defective goods;

　(g)　preventing the exclusion or restriction of liability for breach of the implied terms of title, correspondence with description and sample, quality and fitness for purpose (e.g., those in the SGA 1979, the SG(IT)A 1973 and the SGSA 1982). These terms are not prohibited in non-consumer sales, but are subject to a reasonableness test.

Schedule 2 to the Act provides a set of guidelines for the application of the reasonableness test (see also s. 11). Although the guidelines are not stated to apply to the other situations where the Act subjects terms to a reasonable-ness test, it can be assumed that similar factors will be relevant. Given the debate about whether reasonableness is the same as fairness (the phrase used by the Directive) the guidelines will be reproduced in full. Schedule 2 provides that regard should be had to any of the following which appear relevant:

(a)    the strength of the bargaining positions of the parties relative to each other, taking into account (among other things) alternative means by which the customer's requirements could have been met;

(b)    whether the customer received an inducement to agree to the term, or in accepting it had an opportunity of entering into a similar contract with other persons, but without having to accept a similar term;

(c)    whether the customer knew or ought reasonably to have known of the existence and extent of the term (having regard, among other things, to any custom of the trade and any previous course of dealing between the parties);

(d)    where the term excludes or restricts any relevant liability if some condition is not complied with, whether it was reasonable at the time of the contract to expect that compliance with that condition would be practicable;

(e)    whether the goods were manufactured, processed or adapted to the special order of the customer.

### Scope of application of the Regulations

The Regulations apply to any term in a contract concluded between a seller or supplier and a consumer where the term has not been individually negotiated (reg. 3(1)). Thus the Regulations only apply to consumer con-tracts.

A consumer is defined as a natural person who, in making a contract to which the Regulations apply, is acting for purposes which are outside his business (reg. 2(1)). The restriction to natural persons means that a company can never be a consumer for the purposes of the Regulations. However, sole traders and partners may fall within the scope of the Regulations if they are acting for purposes which are outside their business. The question remains, when are they acting outside their business? Clearly if they buy a kettle to use at home they are, but what if they buy one for their office? It is likely that the same approach will be taken as under the UCTA 1977, namely, that the phrase 'in the course of a business' refers only to activities which are an integral part of the business (see *R & B Customs Brokers Co. Ltd* v *United*

*Dominions Trust Ltd* [1988] 1 WLR 321). So the business person would be acting as a consumer, unless the transactions were conducted with a degree of regularity. Thus a sole trader might be a consumer when buying a kettle for the office, but not a consumer when buying computer equipment which is regularly replaced.

Regulation 2(1) also defines 'seller' as 'a person who sells goods and who, in making a contract to which these Regulations apply, is acting for purposes relating to his business' and 'supplier' as 'a person who supplies goods or services and who, in making a contract to which these Regulations apply, is acting for purposes relating to his business'. Thus the Regulations cover all contracts for the sale or supply of goods or services. The scope of the definitions of seller and supplier appears to be wider than the definition of consumer to the extent that the seller or supplier's purposes in making a contract do not have to be inside the business of the seller or supplier: it is sufficient if they relate to the business. Thus, arguably, almost any contract made in a business capacity will be covered, including, for example, selling the office kettle.

In many pieces of consumer legislation the distinction between consumer and non-consumer sales is drawn by reference to whether one party is acting in the course of business and the other is not. The meaning of 'business' is left largely undefined and indeed the Regulations merely provide the customary vague statement that '"business" includes a trade or profession and the activities of any government department or local or public authority' (reg. 2(1)). It leaves open several questions: for instance, whether charities are businesses? Presumably they will be caught when undertaking trading activity. Are school bazaars covered? Also what about individuals who sell goods occasionally, e.g., amateur bee-keepers selling off honey. However, persons trading on such a small scale are unlikely to use terms which have not been individually negotiated.

Besides being a contract between a seller or supplier and a consumer, the other requirement for the application of the Regulations is that the term which is challenged as being unfair should not have been individually negotiated. The burden of proof is placed on the seller or supplier to show that it was individually negotiated (reg. 3(5)). A term will always be regarded as not having been individually negotiated where it has been drafted in advance and the consumer has not been able to influence the substance of the term (reg. 3(3)).

A standard-form contract is the most obvious case for the application of the Regulations. But do the Regulations apply only to terms which have not been individually negotiated and which are in standard-form contracts? In fact the Regulations and the Directive can be criticised for being unclear on this point. Regulation 3(1) does not seem to require there to be a standard-form contract, merely a term which has not been individually negotiated. Indeed art. 3(2) of the Directive, the equivalent of reg. 3(3), explains the rationale for treating terms drafted in advance as being not individually negotiated, as being that the consumer has not been able to influence the substance of the term. It then goes on to state that this is particularly so in the context of pre-formulated standard contracts, but does not appear to limit the application of the rules to this type of contract. Confusion is created by the next indent of the article in the Directive, which is transposed into reg. 3(4) which states:

Notwithstanding that a specific term or certain aspects of it in a contract has been individually negotiated, these Regulations shall apply to the rest of a contract if an overall assessment of the contract indicates that it is a pre-formulated standard contract.

This seemed to be a way of ensuring that consumer protection was not lost simply because one term was negotiated in an otherwise pre-formulated standard contract. This assumes, however, that the Regulations apply only to standard-form contracts. It would be strange if a provision intended to prevent consumers losing protection by closing a loophole could be used to impose an additional requirement which consumers need to satisfy before they qualify for the Regulations' protection. There is clearly an inconsistency here. If a pre-formulated standard form is required it is strange that there is no definition of that term. It cannot be limited to contracts actually signed by consumers, for recital 11 of the preamble to the Directive makes it clear that the rules are intended to apply equally to oral as well as written contracts, though it could be that the only oral contracts covered are those which expressly incorporate standard conditions. However, there seems no reason why the rules should be limited by a restriction that there be a pre-formulated standard form. Take a hotelier, who did not have a pre-formulated standard form, but had a notice at the reception desk which incorporated into all contracts a term denying liability for goods lost, stolen or damaged whilst in the hotel. Should this not be capable of being challenged under the Regulations? Equally sellers and suppliers may have terms which they draft in advance, but which they do not use all the time. For instance, a car dealer may offer different levels of warranty on second-hand cars or creditors may alter the security, repayment or default rules depending upon the status of the borrower or the purpose for which the loan is used.

No assessment will be made of the fairness of the so-called 'core provisions' of the contract (reg. 3(2)). These include any term which:

(a)  defines the main subject-matter of the contract, or

(b)  concerns the adequacy of the price or remuneration, as against the goods or services sold or supplied.

The purpose of this provision is not to interfere unnecessarily in market-derived contractual outcomes. Thus the parties are free to determine the value of the bargain themselves. It is unfairness derived from the terms which surround that central bargain which the Regulations seek to regulate. Presumably the reasoning is that consumers may fail to recognise the significance of these other terms.

The exclusion of terms relating to price or remuneration is straightforward. It would cover not only the basic price, but also other elements such as taxes, delivery charges and installation costs. On the other hand deciding which terms define the main subject-matter of the contract may be more difficult to ascertain. It may be difficult to distinguish between terms which define the limits of the obligations the seller or supplier undertakes and those which place limitations, restrictions or exclusions on the seller or supplier's obligations. Take a clause in an insurance contract for a bicycle which only covers thefts when the bicycle was in a garage. Does this define the obligation as insuring the bicycle when in the garage or does it restrict the obligation of insuring the bicycle, by excluding liability where it is not in the garage? Whether a term defines the main subject-matter or not may well be a matter of how the contract is drafted. Before lawyers become too eager to start redrafting their clients' contracts they should bear in mind that the courts have under the UCTA 1977 been astute to prevent the purpose of that legislation from being undermined by technical questions of how the terms were presented (see *Smith v Eric S. Bush* [1990] 1 AC 831; *Stewart Gill Ltd v Horatio Myer and Co. Ltd* [1992] QB 600; *Phillips Products Ltd v Hyland* [1987] 1 WLR 659; cf. *Thompson v T. Lohan (Plant Hire) Ltd* [1987] 1 WLR 649).

Note that the protection from scrutiny of the 'core provisions' applies only if they are in plain, intelligible language. Thus if an exclusion from a contract is not clearly explained, or an element of the price is not clearly mentioned, then the term can be challenged (on the construction of written contracts see page 51). Although the core provisions cannot be assessed for fairness themselves, this does not prevent them being taken into account when assessing the fairness of other terms. Thus a limitation of liability, in, say, a photographic processing contract, might be justified where a cheap service is being offered, but not where the charges are extremely high. The ability to take core provisions into account when assessing the fairness of other terms is not expressly mentioned in the Regulations, but is provided for in recital 19 of the preamble to the Directive.

**Unfair terms**

Central to the Regulations is the definition of an unfair term. Regulation 4(1)
defines this as:

> . . . any term which contrary to the requirement of good faith causes a
> significant imbalance in the parties' rights and obligations under the
> contract to the detriment of the consumer.

This seems to impose three hurdles which a consumer has to clear before a
term is labelled unfair. A term must (a) be included contrary to the
requirement of good faith, (b) cause a significant imbalance in the parties'
rights and obligations, and (c) be to the detriment of the consumer. The view
of these as three distinct elements seems to be supported by the DTI which
has stated 'The test of fairness in the Directive has three elements (contrary
to the requirements of good faith, causing a significant imbalance in the
parties' rights and obligations, and to the detriment of the consumer)'
(Further Consultation Document, p. 3). However, clear interrelationships
between the elements will be noted.

*Detriment to the consumer*

The third requirement — that the term be to the detriment of the consumer
— is perhaps the most straightforward to explain. The requirement that the
term be to the consumer's detriment serves to prevent sellers and suppliers
from relying on the Regulations, whilst detriment simply prevents terms
which are actually beneficial to consumers from being challenged. This may
be thought to be self-evident. However, an interesting point arises as to the
time when detriment is to be assessed. A term may have been potentially to
the consumer's detriment at the time the contract was made, but may not
actually be detrimental as events unfolded. For instance, a term might have
allowed the seller or supplier to terminate the contract for a minor infraction
on the consumer's part. This may be thought to be unfair, but what if, as
events turn out, the consumer is quite happy for the contract to be terminated
or even was about to terminate it personally, with possibly more serious
consequences? It may be unlikely that such a scenario would reach the courts
as it is difficult to foresee why a consumer would litigate a term which had
not caused him or her hardship. It is more likely that consumers will seek to
challenge a term which was apparently fair when drafted, but is unfair in the
particular circumstances affecting the consumer. For instance, a clause in a
holiday insurance contract requiring all thefts to be reported to the police

within 24 hours may be generally reasonable, but be unfair if the loss occurs when on a walking expedition two days' trek away from any form of civilisation. Similarly limitation of liability clauses may have appeared fair when drafted, but as events unfold prove to be unduly burdensome on consumers. Whereas justice would seem to require the terms which actually cause injustice to be found to be unfair and terms which cause no hardship not to be found to be unfair, the Regulations seem to lead to the opposite conclusions. This is because reg. 4(2), which we will consider in detail in a moment, refers to the taking into account of the circumstances and terms of the contract *as at the time of the conclusion of the contract*. This seems to require the assessment to be based on the term as of the moment the contract was concluded and not to take subsequent events into account. The DTI was a little opaque on this point, stating: 'The drafting has been amended to make it clear that fairness is to be assessed by referring back to the circumstances at the time of the conclusion of the contract, not that it must be assessed at that time' (Further Consultation Document, p. 16). The first part of the sentence accords with the understanding of the law as stated above, but what is to be made of the statement that it need not be assessed at that time. It could, and perhaps was intended to, mean simply that the assessment could be made when a problem arose and was litigated, but this is so obvious that it beggars belief that it was thought fit to state such an obvious point in an official document. It could mean that although the circumstances and terms are taken into account as at the time of the conclusion of the contract the assessment can also take into account subsequent events. This is perhaps reading too much into a comment in the consultation document, and this latter interpretation would not seem to be consistent with the commonly understood meaning of the Directive.

*A dual procedural and substantive test? The concept of good faith*

The relationship between the good faith and significant imbalance require-ments is the most tantalising in the Regulations. Good faith appears to be a procedural requirement and significant imbalance a substantive standard. However, the matter cannot be conclusively resolved until content is given to the requirements, in particular, to the good faith concept. Outside special contracts, such as insurance law, where there is the concept of contracting in the utmost 'good faith', the good faith concept is alien to English contract law. It is more familiar to Continental lawyers. The French, for instance, talk about the need for '*bonne foi*' and the Germans have the concept of '*Treu und Glauben*'. Thus if the matter comes before the European Court of Justice it is likely to look for inspiration in the legal systems which are conversant with the concept. However, even in the countries which have a similar concept its content seems to be uncertain and flexible.

There are several reasons for supposing that good faith has a procedural content. First, the scope of the Regulations is limited to terms which have not been individually negotiated. This suggests that the mischief lies in the fact that the consumer has been unable to influence the content of the contract, rather than with any desire to control the content of the contract itself. It is conceivable that the Regulations leave the parties free to agree to the most objectionable and unfair terms so long as they result from a fair and open bargaining process. Secondly, reg. 4(3) provides that in determining whether a term satisfies good faith, regard shall be had to the matters in sch. 2 to the Regulations. Schedule 2 refers to matters relating to the way the bargain was struck (see page 43). Thirdly, if there was no procedural content to good faith why do the Regulations not simply provide controls on terms which cause a significant imbalance, without referring to this imbalance having been caused contrary to the requirement of good faith?

Therefore, it would appear to be going too far to read reg. 4(1) in such a way that good faith was equated with entering into a contract with a significant imbalance. In other words it would not appear sufficient to base a finding that a seller or supplier was acting contrary to the requirement of good faith on the fact alone that the contract contained a term which caused a significant imbalance to the consumer's detriment. If such a reading were possible then it would be necessary to ask whether the seller or supplier would be judged objectively or subjectively, i.e., would it only be a breach of the good faith requirement if the seller or supplier was aware (or ought to have been aware) of the significant imbalance?

However, is it possible that the good faith concept is devoid of any substantive content? Take, for example, the inclusion of a term excluding liability for death and personal injury caused by the seller or supplier's negligence. Even if this clause is included with all propriety, for instance, it is clearly written and prominently displayed in the contract and perhaps the consumer's attention is even drawn to the term — could it not be argued that there are some terms which can never be included in good faith in consumer contracts? This is an open question but surely the answer ought to be that some terms can never be included in good faith in consumer contracts. Examples of such terms might be those automatically void in consumer contracts under the UCTA 1977. This could either be rationalised as good faith having a substantive content or that the inclusion of a blatantly unfair term might lead the courts to presume that there must have been some breach of good faith somewhere along the line.

*Criteria for assessing good faith*

Schedule 2 to the Regulations provides that:

> In making an assessment of good faith, regard shall be had in particular to—
>
> (a)  the strength of the bargaining positions of the parties;
>
> (b)  whether the consumer had an inducement to agree to the term;
>
> (c)  whether the goods or services were sold or supplied to the special order of the consumer, and
>
> (d)  the extent to which the seller or supplier has dealt fairly and equitably with the consumer.

These are similar to the guidelines on reasonableness contained in the UCTA 1977, sch. 2, which are reproduced at page 36. In fact items (a), (b) and (c) would appear to have direct counterparts in the UCTA 1977. Item (d) has no direct counterpart, but would seem to cover at least the requirement under the reasonableness guidelines that the consumer must know or ought reasonably to have known of the existence and extent of the term.

It is worthwhile considering the factors to be taken into account when assessing good faith in more detail. Note, however, that they only have to be taken into account and no one factor is likely to be decisive.

The relative strength of the bargaining positions is likely to be one of the most important. However, it is not the fact that one party has superior bargaining power which is important, but rather the fact that the superior position is abused. This is evident from the fact that breach of good faith must be coupled with substantive injustice in the sense of the term causing a significant imbalance. Also, as the 'core provisions' are excluded from the scope of the Regulations the fact that a stronger party can drive a hard bargain is not in itself capable of being challenged. What can be challenged is if that bargain includes terms which are unfair. One might surmise that the abusive element of these terms might be due either to (a) unfair surprise, e.g., a term allowing for unlilateral variation in price, whose potential impact most consumers would not comprehend or (b) monopoly power, e.g., where in order to obtain the goods or services the consumer is forced to accept exclusion clauses as no alternative sellers or suppliers offer the goods or services without these clauses.

Where a consumer has been offered an inducement to agree to a term then this might prevent a prima facie unfair term from being condemned as unfair. For instance, a photo-processing company might offer a cheap service limiting its liability to the price of a replacement film and a higher-priced service with full liability. The inducement need not, however, be restricted to a comparison with the business's own alternatives. Thus a processing company offering a limited liability service could point to the inducement of a cheaper price compared to its competitors. The inducement need not be restricted to price, however. A business might, for instance, offer a faster than normal service, but as a trade-off not guarantee the same quality as under its standard conditions. One must be careful, however. It is unlikely that cheapness or speed of service will be accepted by the courts as an excuse for providing shoddy goods or services. The courts are also likely to be looking for evidence that the consumer was aware that the inducement was linked to the acceptance of what would otherwise have been an unfair term.

How does the fact that the goods were sold or supplied to the consumer's special order influence the assessment of good faith? Presumably the answer lies in the fact that as such goods or services are likely to be less easily resold sellers and suppliers should be given greater freedom to protect themselves, e.g., by limiting the right of rejection. The fact that the goods are sold to special order is only one factor to be taken into account and would not justify unfair terms not related to the particularity of the goods. It would be dangerous to give this factor too wide a scope for many goods can be considered to be sold or supplied to the special order of the consumer and yet this often does not mean the consumer in such transactions is in any better position to protect him or herself.

The requirement that the seller or supplier should have dealt fairly and equitably with the consumer is open to various interpretations. The Directive's preamble, in recital 16, seems to give this factor a higher status. Rather than a factor to be taken into account when assessing good faith it states, '. . . the requirement of good faith may be satisfied by the seller or supplier where he deals fairly and equitably with the other party whose legitimate interests he has to take into account'. Thus dealing fairly and equitably was equated to good faith itself, although the additional factor of consumers having legitimate interests which must be taken into account was added. This gets one little further since one still needs to know what is meant by fair and equitable dealing. It is likely that it was included as a catch-all provision and thus would cover matters such as the extent to which there had been disclosure of the term. Whether the consumer knew or ought to know of the existence and extent of the term was a factor included in the UCTA 1977 guidelines on reasonableness, but it is not expressly mentioned in the Regulations. It could presumably be caught by the reference to fair and equitable dealing. Does the reference to fair and equitable dealing go further than simply requiring disclosure? Does it, for instance, require that the nature and effects of onerous terms be explained to consumers? In other words, instead of a passive disclosure requirement does fair and equitable dealing require sellers and suppliers to assure themselves that consumers know what they are letting themselves in for? It is probably going too far to suggest obligations even beyond the duty to counsel, but a very radical interpretation of the fair and equitable dealing requirement would require a business to refuse to contract with a consumer on terms it knew were disadvantageous to the consumer, even if the consumer was aware of, and willing to accept, the dangers involved.

*Significant imbalance*

The substantive element of the unfairness test is the requirement that the breach of good faith cause a significant imbalance in the parties' rights and obligations under the contract. The requirement that the imbalance be significant is presumably to filter out terms which are only marginally unfair. The assessment of imbalance is likely to be a complex matter. Many terms taken in isolation could be considered unbalanced, but the important question is whether in the overall context of the contract the term is unfair. Regulation 4(2) requires that all the other terms of the contract or of dependent contracts are taken into account.

*The indicative and illustrative list of unfair terms*

Schedule 3 to the Regulations contains what it describes as an indicative and illustrative list of terms which may be regarded as unfair. The status of this list, which is lifted from the annex to the Directive, is uncertain. Regulation 4(4) describes it as an indicative and non-exhaustive list. The fact that the list is non-exhaustive means that other terms not found in sch. 3 can be challenged as unfair. The description of the sch. 3 list as 'indicative' seems to indicate that although these terms are of the sort which will typically be found to be unfair, they will not automatically be held to be unfair since the circumstances of the particular case may justify their inclusion. Schedule 3 is probably best described as a 'greylist' (as opposed to a 'blacklist' of terms which are always held to be unfair). It is perhaps regrettable that the burden of proof was not expressly placed on the seller or supplier to justify the term under challenge, although in practice this is likely to be the effect where a term is challenged which is identical or similar to one included in the schedule.

An analysis of the terms found in the schedule shows that the notion of imbalance is taken seriously. They are concerned predominantly with situations where the seller or supplier has rights over the consumer with the

consumer having no similar rights or the consumer has obligations without
the seller or supplier having any corresponding duties. The terms listed also
show a respect for the exclusion of the 'core provisions'. Rather than
addressing the central elements of the bargain they tend to concentrate on
terms which give the seller or supplier unfair control of the relationship once
the contract has been concluded, e.g., should it be continued or terminated?
What amounts to a breach? What are the consequences of breach? Who
resolves disputes?

In order to make sense of the terms I made the following categorisation
(in *Welfarism in Contract Law* (Aldershot: Dartmouth, 1994) with R.
Brownsword and T. Wilhelmsson) which still appears to be a sensible
rationalisation. In the following the wording of the terms is the same as used
in sch. 3, para. 1.

(a)  *Terms giving one party control over the contract terms or the
performance of the contract.* This covers terms which have the object or
effect of:

(i)      irrevocably binding the consumer to terms with which he had no
real opportunity of becoming acquainted before the conclusion of the
contract (para. 1(i));

(ii)     enabling the seller or supplier to alter the terms of the contract
unilaterally without a valid reason which is specified in the contract (para.
1(j));

(iii)    enabling the seller or supplier to alter unilaterally without a valid
reason any characteristics of the product or service to be provided (para.
1(k));

(iv)     providing for the price of goods to be determined at the time of
delivery or allowing a seller of goods or supplier of services to increase their
price without in both cases giving the consumer the corresponding right to
cancel the contract if the final price is too high in relation to the price agreed
when the contract was concluded (para. 1(l));

(v)      giving the seller or supplier the right to determine whether the
goods or services supplied are in conformity with the contract, or giving him
the exclusive right to interpret any term of the contract (para. 1(m));

(vi)     giving the seller or supplier the possibility of transferring his
rights and obligations under the contract, where this may serve to reduce the
guarantees for the consumer, without the latter's agreement (para. 1(p)).

(b)  *Terms which govern the duration of the contract.* This covers terms
which have the object or effect of:

(i)    enabling the seller or supplier to terminate a contract of indeterminate duration without reasonable notice except where there are serious grounds for doing so (para. 1(g));

(ii)    automatically extending a contract of fixed duration where the consumer does not indicate otherwise, when the deadline fixed for the consumer to express this desire not to extend the contract is unreasonably early (para. 1(h)).

(c)    *Terms which prevent the parties having equal rights.* This covers terms which have the object or effect of:

(i)    making an agreement binding on the consumer whereas provision of services by the seller or supplier is subject to a condition whose realisation depends on his own will alone (para. 1(c));

(ii)    permitting the seller or supplier to retain sums paid by the consumer where the latter decides not to conclude or perform the contract, without providing for the consumer to receive compensation of an equivalent amount from the seller or supplier where the latter is the party cancelling the contract (para. 1(d));

(iii)    authorising the seller or supplier to dissolve the contract on a discretionary basis where the same facility is not granted to the consumer, or permitting the seller or supplier to retain the sums paid for services not yet supplied by him where it is the seller or supplier himself who dissolves the contract (para. 1(f));

(iv)    obliging the consumer to fulfil all his obligations where the seller or supplier does not perform his (para. 1(o)).

(d)    *Exclusion, limitation and penalty clauses.* This covers terms which have the object or effect of:

(i)    excluding or limiting the legal liability of a seller or supplier in the event of the death of a consumer or personal injury to the latter resulting from an act or omission of that seller or supplier (para. 1(a));

(ii)    inappropriately excluding or limiting the legal rights of the consumer *vis-à-vis* the seller or supplier or another party in the event of total or partial non-performance or inadequate performance by the seller or supplier of any of the contractual obligations, including the option of offsetting a debt owed to the seller or supplier against any claim which the consumer may have against him (para. 1(b));

(iii)    requiring any consumer who fails to fulfil his obligations to pay a disproportionately high sum in compensation (para. 1(e));

(iv)   limiting the seller's or supplier's obligation to respect commitments undertaken by his agents or making his commitments subject to compliance with a particular formality (para. 1(n));

(v)   excluding or hindering the consumer's right to take legal action or exercise any other legal remedy, particularly by requiring the consumer to take disputes exclusively to arbitration not covered by legal provisions, unduly restricting the evidence available to him or imposing on him a burden of proof which, according to the applicable law, should lie with another party to the contract (para. 1(q)).

*Special cases: financial services*

The financial services sector failed to have itself excluded from the Directive. Several of the indicatively unfair terms could be construed as threatening terms which are legitimately included in financial services contracts. Schedule 3, para. 2, therefore includes certain concessions to the financial services industry, as well as seeking to ensure that certain other frequently used legitimate terms can continue. Often the purpose is simply to state expressly that a term is valid when the same conclusion could have been reached by a sensible interpretation of the wording in the indicative list. The particularity with which these safeguards have been drawn up might lead one to conclude that the list in para. 1 was only formally a greylist and in practice a blacklist. These clarifications should, however, probably be read simply as an attempt to assuage the fears of particularly strong lobby groups. The following clarifications to the scope of sch. 3, para. 1 are made:

(a)   The fact that para. 1(g) prevents the seller or supplier terminating a contract of indeterminate duration without reasonable notice unless there are serious grounds, does not prevent the supplier of financial services from terminating such a contract without notice provided there is a valid reason and the term requires the supplier to inform the other contracting party or parties immediately (sch. 3, para. 2(a)). There must be a valid reason, but it need not be a serious reason.

(b)   The prohibition in para. 1(j) on unilateral alterations without a valid reason does not prevent—

(i)   suppliers of financial services from altering interest rates or other charges provided there is a valid reason and so long as the other party is informed of them at the earliest opportunity and the other is free to dissolve the contract immediately (sch. 3, para. 2(b)). In some respects this proviso is actually more stringent than para. 1(j), since in addition to the requirement that there is a valid reason the other party must be informed and given the opportunity to dissolve the contract. This could cause problems for lenders with variable interest rates if it means that after each increase the consumer is given the option of being released from the contract.

(ii)     There is a general exemption from para. 1(j), not restricted to the financial services industry, for all contracts of indeterminate duration, provided the consumer is informed with reasonable notice of any unilateral alteration of contract conditions and is given the chance to dissolve the contract (sch. 3, para. 2(b)).

(c)     The prohibition in para. 1(l), on terms which allow sellers or suppliers to increase their prices without giving the consumer the right to cancel if the final price is too high, is without prejudice to the use of price indexation clauses provided such a clause is itself lawful and the method by which the prices vary is explicitly described (sch. 3, para. (2)(d)).

(d)     Subparagraphs (g), (j) and (l) of para. 1 do not apply to:

(i)     transactions in transferable securities, financial instruments and other products and services where the price is linked to fluctuations in a stock exchange quotation or index or a financial market rate that the seller or supplier does not control; and

(ii)     contracts for the purchase or sale of foreign currency, traveller's cheques or international money orders denominated in foreign currency (sch. 3, para. 2(c)).

*Factors to be taken into account in assessing the unfair nature of a term*

Factors relevant to the assessment of good faith have been considered in detail (see page 43). Attention will now be paid to reg. 4(2), which provides for certain factors to be taken into account when assessing whether a term is unfair. Three such factors can be discerned from reg. 4(2), namely;

(a)     the nature of the goods or services for which the contract was concluded;

(b)     the circumstances attending the conclusion of the contract; and

(c)     all the other terms of the contract or of another contract on which it is dependent.

The wording of reg. 4(2) is not free of ambiguity. Whilst factor (a) is to be taken account of, the assessment of unfairness shall be made with reference, as at the time of the conclusion of the contract, to factors (b) and (c). Quite what the difference is between 'taking into account' a factor and having reference to a factor is unclear. It is also uncertain whether the restriction on the time for assessment, as being the time the contract was concluded, only refers to factor (b) and not (c). Such a limited interpretation would appear implausible given that the circumstances attending the conclusion of the contract would in any event always seem to have to be assessed at the time of the conclusion of the contract, unless such a restrictive interpretation was intended to have the limited objective of seeking to exclude factors which existed but were not known to the parties at the time the contract was concluded. However, it is likely that the time of assessment was meant to govern both factors (b) and (c). It might, however, have been clearer if it had simply been stated that the assessment of the unfair nature of the term would be assessed as at the time of the conclusion of the contract.

*Individual and collective assessment of fairness*

Below (see page 52), it will be explained that there are two ways an unfair term can be challenged: by an individual who wants not to be bound by an unfair term and by the Director General of Fair Trading (hereafter Director General) seeking an injunction. This is problematic because the same test of unfairness is applied to both individual and collective redress mechanisms. Yet many of the factors, e.g., the strength of the bargaining position of the parties and the circumstances attending the conclusion of the contract only seem appropriate when assessing a term in the context of a particular occasion on which a contract was made. Indeed the scope of the collective redress mechanism might be thought to be limited as it could apply fairly only to terms which could not be conceived of as ever being fair under any circumstances.

*Relationship with the Unfair Contract Terms Act 1977*

Many would have preferred the Regulations to have been integrated into the scheme of the UCTA 1977. It was not, so people are likely to ask what the relationship is between these two pieces of legislation.

The UCTA 1977 prohibits certain terms altogether, e.g., exclusions of liability for negligence causing personal injury and death and exclusion of implied quality terms in consumer contracts. In contrast the Regulations do not exclude any terms *per se*, but those prohibited by the UCTA 1977 are covered by the indicative list of unfair terms and it will be hard, if not impossible, for a seller or supplier to show that such a term could be used in good faith.

For terms favouring the seller or supplier, but which are not automatically prohibited under the UCTA 1977, the path to challenging the term requires the consumer to demonstrate that its inclusion was unreasonable. Under the Regulations a term which is significantly imbalanced to the consumer's detriment must be shown to be contrary to the requirement of good faith. Is there a difference between unreasonableness and lack of good faith? The DTI took the view that whilst:

> . . . a similar result is in most cases likely to be achieved when applying the test of fairness in the Directive as when the term is considered to determine whether it is reasonable under the Act, there can be no guarantee that this would be the case. There may be terms which would be contrary to the requirement of good faith but would be reasonable, and there may be others which would not be contrary to the requirement of good faith and yet are unreasonable. (Further Consultation Document, p.12.)

Such instances might be more possible to imagine if unreasonableness under the UCTA 1977 was a purely substantive concept. In fact the guidelines on reasonableness address the same type of procedural fairness questions as the guidelines on good faith. Thus, whilst it is possible that a particular term would be caught by one concept and not the other, this is unlikely. However, although there are some court decisions applying the unreasonableness concept, there are none as yet applying the good faith test. Until the scope of the good faith test is settled, and remember this must be interpreted in the light of its European origin, the relationship between the UCTA 1977 and the Regulations cannot be settled.

**Construction of written contracts**

Regulation 6 requires that sellers and suppliers ensure that any written term of a contract is expressed in plain, intelligible language. A weakness is that no sanction is provided for breach of this obligation, which in any event may be difficult to control as persons may legitimately disagree on what constitutes plain, intelligible language. By whose standards should the contract language be judged? Should it be plain and intelligible to the lawyer, a well-educated consumer, an average consumer, the particular consumer? An indirect sanction is provided by the provision that if there is doubt about the meaning of a written term, the interpretation most favourable to the consumer shall prevail.

**Enforcement**

The Regulations provide for two forms of redress against the use of unfair terms in consumer contracts. A consumer who has concluded a contract containing an unfair term can ask the court to find that the unfair term should not be binding on him or her (reg. 5(1)). The remainder of the contract will continue to bind the parties, if it is capable of continuing in existence without the unfair term (reg. 5(2)). This is the same approach as under the UCTA 1977. The novel feature of the Regulations is the power of the Director General to seek injunctions against unfair terms. The Consumers' Association had argued that it should be given the right to bring actions on behalf of consumers. The restriction of the right of action to the Director General would appear to be adequate to meet the obligations of the Directive which talked of providing for action to be taken by 'persons or organizations, having a legitimate interest under national law in protecting consumers'. In other European countries, such as France and Germany, there is a tradition of granting standing in such actions to consumer organisations, but the Directive seems intentionally worded so as to allow member States freedom to choose methods of collective protection of consumers which suit their own traditions.

*Procedure*

The Director General's powers are activated only when there has been a complaint (reg. 8(1)). He would appear to have no power to act on his own initiative, although he could presumably suggest to appropriate persons or bodies that he would welcome complaints on a certain matter. There would seem to be no limitation on who can complain. Private individuals, trading standards departments and consumer organisations would all appear to be free to complain. In fact, consumer groups may find this procedure, whereby the Director General is required to investigate their complaints, more beneficial than having the right of action themselves, but inadequate resources to utilise it.

The European Commission in its green paper, *Access of Consumers to Justice and the Settlement of Consumer Disputes in the Single Market* (COM(93) 576) considered ways of promoting consumer protection through the use of injunctions by public authorities and consumer organisations. It noted that under the United Kingdom's Fair Trading Act 1973 the Director General had no powers to deal with conduct affecting consumers in other member States if it was not detrimental to the interests of consumers in the United Kingdom. Although the idea of free movement of injunctions within the Community is still some way off, nevertheless the Director General would appear to be able to entertain complaints from foreign consumers, consumer organisations and public authorities. If the Director General tried to argue that it was not appropriate for him to bring proceedings as no United Kingdom consumers were affected, this is likely to be treated as a breach of the United Kingdom's obligations under art. 7(1) of the Directive to ensure that adequate and effective means exist to prevent the continued use of unfair terms.

The Director General is under a duty to consider any complaint unless it appears frivolous or vexatious (reg. 8(1)). Having considered the complaint, the Director General then has a discretion as to whether to bring proceedings for an injunction against any person appearing to him to be using or recommending the use of an unfair term in contracts concluded with consumers (reg. 8(2)). In these proceedings he may also apply for an interlocutory injunction. In reaching this decision he may have regard to any undertakings provided (reg. 8(3)). However, he must give reasons for his decision to apply or not to apply for an injunction (reg. 8(4)). These Regulations have the potential to overburden the Director General's Office of Fair Trading. It is possible that the Director General could use limited resources as an excuse for not proceeding with actions against all but the most serious unfair terms.

Proceedings for an injunction, including an interlocutory injunction, can be brought against any person appearing to the Director General to be using or recommending the use of unfair terms. Thus action could be brought against not only sellers and suppliers, but also manufacturers, franchisors and, most significantly, trade associations which recommend the use of unfair terms in standard forms. The injunction may relate not only to the use of a term in a particular contract but to any similar term, or a term having like effect, used or recommended for use in consumer contracts (reg. 8(6)). Therefore a term could be prohibited from being used in a variety of contracts, and attempts to avoid the effect of the injunction by drafting clauses in a different manner to achieve the same result as the prohibited clause will be caught.

The court may grant an injunction on such terms as it thinks fit (reg. 8(5)). It is unclear whether the court has the freedom to consider for itself whether the term is unfair or whether it simply has to accept the Director General's view, subject to administrative law requirements that the decision be a reasonable one. The discretionary way in which the court's powers are framed and the fact that the assessment of a term is a mixed question of fact and law would appear to permit the court to make its own assessment of the fairness or otherwise of the term. This discretion also allows the court to decide, for instance, which particular terms are caught and whether the injunction should apply only to an individual, to a whole industry or to all businesses. The injunction may relate to a particular contract term drawn up for general use and a similar term, or one having like effect, which is used or recommended for use by any party to the proceedings (reg. 8(6)).

A difficulty, already alluded to, with this injunction procedure is that the standard being applied is, at least in formal terms, the same as when an individual consumer challenges an unfair term. Yet different judgments must be made when a term is being prohibited outright. For an injunction to be granted, one would have thought, there must be no circumstances in which the term could have been used in a manner prohibited by the injunction and yet be fair. For extreme clauses such as exclusions of death and personal injury caused by negligence it may be possible for an injunction to be granted in broad terms. Indeed many of the clauses which might be considered capable of justifying an outright ban are those which are absolutely prohibited by the UCTA 1977. The fairness of most clauses, however, depends upon the circumstances surrounding the conclusion of the contract and the overall contract package: this would favour rather narrowly drawn injunctions. Although the individual injunctions may be narrowly drawn, this does not prevent them from having precedent value, which should make it easier for the Director General to obtain undertakings in similar cases in the future.

The Director General is empowered to arrange for the dissemination of information and advice concerning the operation of these Regulations to the general public and to all persons likely to be affected. Thus guidance booklets on the operation of the scheme can be published. Whether information and advice concerning the operation of the scheme goes so far as to allow the Director General to publicise undertakings and injunctions is a moot point. The operation of the scheme could be construed as being limited to the mechanics of the scheme rather than the results it produces. Such publicity would also appear to be outside the Director General's general powers to publicise consumer matters contained in the Fair Trading Act 1973, s. 124.

*Choice of laws*

So long as a contract has a close connection with the territory of the member States of the EEA, the Regulations shall apply to it notwithstanding any contract term which purports to apply the law of a non-member State (reg. 7). This seeks to prevent the Regulations from being circumvented by the use of choice of law clauses designating the law of a non-member State as the applicable law.

# 5

## General Product Safety Regulations 1994

### Background

Part II of the Consumer Protection Act 1987 (hereafter CPA 1987) provides a fairly comprehensive scheme for regulaing product safety. In addition to regulation-making powers (including emergency powers), there is a general safety duty, and breach of the regulations or general safety duty is a criminal offence. These provisions are supported by giving the Secretary of State the power to issue notices prohibiting the supply of unsafe goods, or to serve notices which require the publication of warnings about unsafe goods. Enforcement authorities can serve suspension notices preventing the supply of goods believed to be unsafe for up to six months and can seek a court order for the forfeiture of goods which fail to comply with the safety provisions. In addition enforcement authorities are given extensive powers to make test purchases, search, inspect records and seize and detain goods suspected of being unsafe.

### EEC Directive

Many European countries did not have as developed a system of regulation to prevent unsafe products reaching the market-place or taking steps to warn consumers of defects in goods which had reached the market-place. The need for a general Directive was becoming apparent given the incomplete coverage of the sectoral Directives and the need to enhance the confidence of consumers in goods which were circulating more freely within the internal market. The jurisprudence of the European Court of Justice on arts 30 to 36 of the Treaty of Rome was making it more difficult for member States to justify consumer protection measures which had the effect of impeding inter-State trade. Thus the general product safety Directive (92/59/EEC, OJ No. L 228/24 of 11.8.92; see appendix 7) was adopted on 29 June 1992 with an implementation date of 29 June 1994. The Directive introduces a general product safety requirement, requires member States to have measures in place to ensure that that objective is achieved and introduces an emergency Community procedure, as well as developing existing procedures for the notification and exchange of information relating to dangerous products. For some countries, such as Germany, Greece, Italy and Portugal, this new Directive required systematic changes to their legal structures and possibly the creation of new administrative agencies. Others, such as France, took the view that their domestic laws already satisfied the obligations created by the Directive. As regards the United Kingdom the Directive does not provide any serious challenge to the existing structures, but it was thought necessary to replace the general safety duty contained in the CPA 1987 with one which extends the scope of the general duty to all the products covered by the Directive and which uses terminology, such as the crucial definition of safety, which is inspired by the Directive.

Thus producers and lawyers in the United Kingdom are faced by new and complex Regulations which create a regime parallel to that created by part II of the Consumer Protection Act 1987. These Regulations are the General Product Safety Regulations 1994, SI 1994/2328 (hereafter GPSR 1994; see appendix 6). They were made on 5 September, laid before Parliament on 8 September and came into force on 3 October 1994. The Regulations were enacted after the time limit permitted by the Directive. It is understood that the delay was due to the time it took to collect cost-compliance information as required by domestic United Kingdom legislation. It is, perhaps, understandable that the officials and minister concerned wanted to wait until this information was collected before introducing the Regulations. However, European law does not accept domestic legislative procedures as an excuse for failing to implement Directives. If someone was injured between 29 June 1994 (the implementation date) and 3 October 1994 (the date the Regulations came into force) by a product which would have been caught by the wider general product safety standard introduced by the Directive, it would be an interesting question whether the United Kingdom government would be liable in damages under the *Francovich* principle (see page 3).

## Scope of the changes

The GPSR 1994 do not repeal the old law, but rather disapply it in specified circumstances. The CPA 1987, s. 10, which imposed the general safety duty, is disapplied, by reg. 5, GPSR 1994 to the extent that it imposed general safety requirements which must be complied with if products are (a) to be placed on the market, offered or agreed to be placed on the market or exposed or possessed to be placed on the market by *producers* or (b) supplied, offered or agreed to be supplied or exposed or possessed to be supplied by *distributors*. The general safety requirement in s. 10, CPA 1987 may retain some life. This is because the CPA 1987 bases regulation on the concept of supply, which is given a broad definition by s. 46 to include (a) selling, hiring out or lending goods; (b) entering into hire-purchase agreements; (c) performing contracts for work and materials; (d) providing goods in exchange for consideration other than money (including trading stamps); (e) providing goods under a statutory function and (f) giving the goods as a prize or otherwise making a gift of the goods. Section 10 may still have some relevance. The Regulations disapply it to *distributors* on criteria which also relate to the concept of supply, but for *producers* the section is disapplied by reference to the concept of 'placing on the market' which may have a narrower meaning than supply, and in particular could arguably not include the hiring and lending of products. The GPSR 1994 do not have a definition of supply, but it would be sensible if the CPA 1987's definition were to be applied.

### 'Producers' and 'distributors'

The definitions of 'producer' and 'distributor' are critical, as the Regulations differentiate between the requirements imposed on producers and distributors. 'Producer' is given a broad definition by reg. 2(1). It covers manufacturers, those who present themselves as manufacturers by affixing their name, trade mark or other distinctive feature to the product and persons who recondition products. Manufacturers are deemed to be producers only if they are established in the European Community, otherwise responsibility is placed on the manufacturer's representative or, if there is no representative established in the Community, the importer. This has the useful objective of making enforcement easier by allowing enforcement authorities to go against someone located in the Community. There may, however, be a lacuna. The assumption is that the importer is someone based in the Community, but it could actually be an overseas entity with no physical presence in the Community. Of course, 'importer' could be given a more purposive interpretation, which is highly likely given the European Court's teleological method of reasoning. Liability could then be imposed on the first party physically located in the Community. It is, perhaps, unfortunate that the importer entirely replaces the manufacturer as the responsible person rather than being an additional defendant the authorities can go against. Consumer protection enforcement would be simplified if authorities were allowed to go against the importer into their own country, but this would undermine the concept of Europe as a single market, which was behind the drafting of the European Directive.

Other professionals in the supply chain will also be producers in so far as their activities may affect the safety properties of a product placed on the market. Therefore only those 'distributors' whose activities do not affect the safety properties of the product are classed as distributors for the purposes of the GPSR 1994. Regulation 2(1) defines 'distributors' as any professionals in the supply chain whose activity does not affect the safety properties of a product.

In many cases distributors in the modern era of pre-packaged goods will not affect the safety properties of goods. One important exception to this is food distributors, whose storage conditions can have a substantial impact on the safety of food. It would also seem to bring others, commonly thought of as distributors, within the definition of producer, for instance, gas installers whose installation of gas appliances affects their safety, and probably also retailers who assemble the final product.

**Products covered**

One reason why the new Regulations will have an impact in the United Kingdom is because the products covered are more extensive than those which fell within the scope of the CPA 1987. 'Product' is defined, in reg. 2(1) of the GPSR 1994 as meaning:

> any product intended for consumers or likely to be used by consumers, supplied whether for consideration or not in the course of a commercial activity and whether new, used or reconditioned; provided, however, a product which is used exclusively in the context of a commercial activity even if it is used for or by a consumer shall not be regarded as a product for the purposes of these Regulations provided always and for the avoidance of doubt this exception shall not extend to the supply of such a product to a consumer.

The CPA 1987 had excluded (a) growing crops; (b) water, food, feeding stuff or fertiliser; (c) gas; (d) aircraft (other than hang-gliders) and motor vehicles; (e) controlled drugs and licensed medicinal products and (f) tobacco. Many of these were regulated by other statutes, but it is interesting to note that the Food Safety Act 1990 had stopped short of imposing a general safety duty and preferred instead to establish more limited food safety requirements. The inclusion of tobacco under the GPSR 1994 may be of some concern to the tobacco industry and smokers who fear that their product is being threatened. However, as we shall see, the definition of a safe product does not require absolute safety, but only the minimum compatible with the product's use which is considered acceptable. This standard may save tobacco from being banned altogether, but high-tar or untipped cigarettes may be challenged and certainly any addictive additive could render the product unsafe. An important extension is that which brings second-hand products within the general safety duty. Second-hand goods supplied as antiques are excluded, however (reg. 3(a)). The Regulations do cover reconditioned goods, but exclude goods supplied for repair or reconditioning before use, provided the supplier makes this clear to the other party (reg. 3(b)).

Part II of the CPA 1987 did not apply to a person who could show that he reasonably believed the goods would not be used or consumed in the United Kingdom. Both the Directive and the Regulations are silent on the question of geographic scope. However, the purpose of the Directive would be frustrated if member States were allowed to sanction the marketing of dangerous products in other member States. Therefore at the very least the phrase 'placing the goods on the market' must mean placing them anywhere within the internal market. What about goods marketed within EFTA countries who have signed up to the European Economic Area Agreement (now of course reduced in size as Austria, Finland and Sweden have joined the Community)? These ought to be treated equally with member States, and this would seem to be the position since reg. 2(2) provides that references to the 'Community' should be treated as references to the European Economic Area. Could a bold interpretation be given to the phrase 'placing goods on the market' so that it included marketing to non-member States or could it be implied that it is only concerned with goods placed on the internal market? The difficulty is to know whether placing on the market is interpreted as a physical act or if marketing is sufficient. It is disappointing that neither the Directive nor the Regulations contain a definition of the phrase 'placing on the market'.

The Regulations apply to any product intended for consumers or likely to be used by consumers, which would seem to be a little wider than the definition of consumer goods in the CPA 1987, s. 10, which talked of goods which are ordinarily intended for private use or consumption. Thus it would seem to include products which are used both by business and consumers, such as building materials. Even if a supplier wishes to restrict supply to professionals the products would seem to be caught if it is apparent that they find their way on to the consumer market.

Uncertainty surrounds the scope of the exclusion of products used exclusively in the context of a commercial activity even if they are used for or by a consumer. The intent seems to be to exclude products such as shampoos which are only supplied to hair salons, railway carriages, super-market trolleys, escalators in shops and ski-lifts, to mention but a few of the examples which have been discussed in this context. This exclusion appears to come from the fifth recital to the Directive which states, 'Whereas production equipment, capital goods and other products used exclusively in the context of a trade or business are not covered by this Directive'. This certainly appears to be narrower, especially in view of the examples cited, than the interpretation some people have given to the exclusion contained in the GPSR 1994. Thus whilst one can see that infrastructure such as escalators, ski-lifts and railway carriages are of a different nature from normal consumer goods, there would seem little reason to exclude shampoo which is directly used on consumers and shopping trolleys which consumers themselves use. The purpose may have been to leave the commercial enterprise to assure the safety of its customer; but the type of goods cited in the preamble seem to illustrate a more sensible distinction between large capital goods and smaller consumer products. The shampoo and the trolley should be covered by the GPSR 1994, as they are products which the consumer uses in a very individualised manner. Further support for this approach might be found by applying the *eiusdem generis* rule to the preamble so that reference to 'other products' must be given a meaning similar to the goods cited, i.e., production equipment and capital goods. Also what is to be made of the fact that the exception made by reg. 2(1) for goods used exclusively in the context of a commercial activity is expressly said 'for the avoidance of doubt' (!!) not to extend to the supply of such a product to a consumer?

### Relationship to vertical regulations

The general product safety Directive should be viewed in context of the general scheme of European regulation of products. In the early years the Community sought detailed product-by-product regulation. There were several drawbacks to these procedures: the negotiations were time-consuming; unanimity was required; producing total harmonisation stifled innovation and regional diversity; it failed to take account of European standardisation work; there continued to be national initiatives which obstructed harmonisation and even where Directives were adopted member States were slow to implement them. A Council Resolution of 7 May 1985 took a new approach to the technical harmonisation of standards (OJ 1985 C 136/1, 4.6.1985). The new-approach Directives attempt on a sectoral basis to set out essential safety requirements, which are then fleshed out by the standard-making bodies. The general product safety Directive is intended to fill the lacunae which existed in the coverage of the vertical legislation. The Directive is rather vague about the relationship between the new horizontal legislation and existing Community vertical legislation. Recital 7 states that '. . . when there are specific rules of Community law, of the total harmonization type, and in particular rules adopted on the basis of the new approach, which lay down obligations regarding product safety, further obligations should not be imposed on economic operators as regards the placing on the market of products covered by such rules'. On one reading such Directives are excluded altogether from the general safety duty, but included as regards post-market controls, which are not provided for in the specific Directives. However, the next recital seems to make it clear that where Community regulation covers only certain aspects of safety or categories of risk then the obligations of economic operators are determined solely by those provisions in respect of those aspects and therefore by implication one can assume other safety aspects are governed by the general product safety Directive. This is the position adopted by the GPSR 1994, which states the provisions apply only in so far as other Community law does not make specific provision governing an aspect of the safety of the product (reg. 4). Admittedly, reg. 3(c) does exclude from the scope of the Regulations any product where there are specific provisions in rules of Community law governing all aspects of the safety of the product, but this makes it clear that all aspects of safety must be covered. If Community law covers all safety aspects then it is self evident that there is no scope for reg. 4 to apply.

**Definition of 'safe product'**

The centre-piece of the GPSR 1994 is the requirement that no producer shall place a product on the market unless the product is a safe product. The definition of 'safe product' is therefore crucial and the Regulations adopt almost word for word the definition contained in the Directive. Regulation 2(1) provides:

'safe product' means any product which, under normal or reasonably foreseeable conditions of use, including duration, does not present any risk or only the minimum risks compatible with the product's use, considered as acceptable and consistent with a high level of protection for the safety and health of persons, taking into account in particular—
(a) the characteristics of the product, including its composition, packaging, instructions for assembly and maintenance;

(b)   the effect on other products, where it is reasonably foreseeable that it will be used with other products;

(c)   the presentation of the product, the labelling, any instructions for its use and disposal and any other indication or information provided by the producer; and

(d)   the categories of consumers at serious risk when using the product, in particular children,

and the fact that higher levels of safety may be obtained or other products presenting a lesser degree of risk may be available shall not of itself cause the product to be considered other than a safe product.

Thus the product must be looked at in the round when assessing its safety. A safe product might be rendered unsafe by its packaging — for example tablets supplied without a childproof lid or baby food sold in a jar without a tamper-proof seal. The packaging can itself also be what makes the product unsafe. Thus in the United States there is currently concern about the five-gallon plastic containers in which produce is supplied in bulk to households. Often they are subsequently used in the garden to collect water, but a number of deaths have occurred from children falling into them and drowning. There have been calls for the containers to be labelled or redesigned to prevent such accidents occurring. Also instructions on assembly or use can render safe a product which would have been unsafe without such guidance. Equally, misleading instructions can make a normally safe product dangerous.

The definition of 'safe product' in the GPSR 1994 is perhaps more objective than the definition of 'defect in a product' in the CPA 1987, s. 3, which refers to the 'safety' which 'persons generally are entitled to expect'. This might reflect the low standards the general public have perhaps come to expect in an era of mass-produced goods. The GPSR 1994 definition is stronger in that it makes it clear that the product should contain no risks or only those compatible with its use. There is some room for subjectivity in that there may be debate about what risks are considered acceptable, but in making this assessment the standard is strengthened by the fact that acceptable risks must also be consistent with a high level of protection for the safety and health of persons. The definition also prevents the producer fixing a very narrow range of uses for the product as a product must be safe under both normal *and* reasonably foreseeable conditions of use. In this respect the definition is wider than the general safety requirement in the CPA 1987, s. 10, which related safety to the purposes for which the product was being marketed. The product can also be unsafe because of its effect on other products, which it is reasonably foreseeable that it will be used with. For instance, an attachment may be dangerous when fitted to a particular model. The new definition can also be seen as being more stringent than that in s. 10, in that account must be taken of categories of consumers at serious risk when using the product. Children are mentioned as a particular at-risk category, but other groups might include the elderly, handicapped or those with serious allergies.

There is a presumption that a product is safe if it conforms to the specific rules of United Kingdom law laying down health and safety requirements (reg. 10(1)). Under s. 10(3)(b)(ii) of the CPA 1987 the Secretary of State had power to approve standards so that compliance with them satisfied the general safety requirement. This power has now been repealed and the Approval of Safety Standards Regulations 1987 (SI 1987/1911) have been revoked (GPSR 1994, reg. 6). Regulation 10(2) provides that where there are no specific rules of the kind referred to in reg. 10(1), safety should be assessed having regard to:

(a)  voluntary United Kingdom national standards giving effect to a European standard (e.g., BSI standards); or

(b)  Community technical specifications (e.g., CEN standards); or

(c)  if there are none of the above, (i) United Kingdom standards, or (ii) codes of good practice in respect of health and safety in the product sector concerned, or (iii) the state of the art and technology.

Account must also be taken of the safety which consumers may reasonably expect.

The fact that higher levels of safety may be obtained, or other products present a lesser degree of risk, shall not of itself cause the product to be considered other than a safe product (reg. 2(1)). This is clearly right for otherwise many common products would be unsafe, for instance, every car without an airbag would always be deemed unsafe. The product needs to be looked at in the round considering all its elements, including price. However, evidence that higher levels of safety could be obtained or that safer products are available, although not conclusive, can be used as evidence to suggest that the product presents more than the minimum acceptable risks.

## Obligations of producers and distributors

The GPSR 1994 follow the Directive in imposing specific requirements on producers (regs. 7 and 8) and distributors (reg. 9). Regulation 7 specifically places an obligation on producers not to place a product on the market unless it is safe. Breach of this obligation is an offence (reg. 12). Regulation 8 places certain obligations on producers to provide and collect information on product risks. Producers must, within the limits of their activities, provide consumers with the relevant information to enable them to assess the risks inherent in a product throughout the normal or reasonably foreseeable period of its use, where such risks are not obvious without adequate warnings, and to take precautions against those risks (reg. 8(1)(a)). Whilst manufacturers might be expected to provide this information, it is by no means clear that this could be expected of someone who became a producer because, for instance, he was responsible for storing the goods. This seems to be provided for by limiting producers' obligations to those 'within the limit of their activities'.

Producers must also, again within the limits of their activities, adopt measures commensurate with the characteristics of the products they supply, to enable them to be informed of the risks which these products might present and to take appropriate action, including, if necessary, withdrawing the product in question from the market to avoid those risks (reg. 8(1)(b)). Where appropriate this may involve marking the products or product batches, sample testing of marketed products, investigating complaints and keeping distributors informed of such monitoring (reg. 8(2)). Again these obligations would not seem appropriate for all those who only technically fall within the definition of producer.

Distributors are under an obligation to act with due care to help ensure producers comply with their obligation under reg. 7 to place only safe products on the market. Without limiting this general obligation, reg. 9 goes on to place two specific obligations on distributors. They must not supply products which they either know are dangerous or should have presumed were dangerous, on the basis of the information in their possession and as a professional (reg. 9(a)). The reference to their knowledge as a professional would seem to provide that distributors are deemed to have constructive knowledge of common knowledge and practice which is known to the profession generally. Breach of this obligation is an offence (reg. 12). In addition, distributors must within the limits of their activities participate in monitoring the safety of products placed on the market, in particular by passing on information on the product risks and cooperating in the action taken to avoid those risks (reg. 9(b)). This looks like imposing on distributors a subsidiary obligation to that owed by producers: whilst producers must inform themselves of the risks, distributors merely have to pass on information on product risks (presumably their obligations would involve passing information both downwards to their customers and back upwards from customer complaints to the producer) and respond to preventative action taken by producers. However, distributors are also said to be under a duty to

act with due care to ensure compliance with the general safety requirement
and the specific obligations mentioned are explicitly stated in reg. 9 to be
without prejudice to that duty of care. What due care requires clearly depends
both upon the degree of danger typically presented by the product in question
and the role played by the distributor in relation to the product. Less might
be expected of a distributor who merely acted as a conduit through which
the goods passed (e.g., a wholesaler) than of a distributor like a retailer, who
has control of the goods at the time they are supplied to the consumer. A
difficult question is whether the size of the distributor should be relevant. If
'due care' was equated to the negligence standard then the size of the
distributor would appear to be irrelevant as tort law assesses fault by
objective standards. Yet that does not make sense and, in case law relating
to the due diligence defence, the precautions which can be expected to be
taken have been related to the size of the enterprise. Thus in *Garrett* v *Boots
Chemists Ltd* (16 July 1980, unreported, but cited in C. J. Miller and B. W.
Harvey, *Consumer and Trading Law Cases and Materials* (London: Butter-
worths, 1985)) it was commented that 'what might be reasonable for a large
retailer might not be reasonable for the village shop' and the court went on
to hold that a company the size of Boots should have taken random samples
of the batches of the pencils which were alleged to be in breach of the Pencils
and Graphic Instruments (Safety) Regulations 1974 (SI 1974/226). This is
significant for it illustrates that due care by distributors might involve
performing some of the tasks imposed on producers relating to informing
themselves of product risks. Distributors would not normally be expected to
provide consumers with information to assess the risks inherent in the
product, but neither would producers unless their activities were such that
they were in a position to be informed of these and to take measures to
ensure the consumer is informed. In other words within the limits of their
respective activities the requirements on producers and distributors would
appear to be almost identical.

The above has proceeded on the assumption that when assessing the due
care expected of a distributor allowance can be made for the size of the
defendant. In terms of the GPSR 1994 this matter may be somewhat
academic. Even if due care ought to be given an objective interpretation, the
GPSR 1994 in any event provide for a due diligence defence (reg. 14) which
would allow the size of the distributor to be taken into account. But what if
the European legislation had intended to impose an objective standard? The
European legislation would then be incorrectly implemented because of the
presence of the due diligence defence. The Department of Trade and Industry
Consultation Document on the draft Regulations stated that the inclusion of
a due diligence defence for the new offences created 'follows the precedent

set by other UK regulations implementing EC product safety legislation' (para. 14). The question might be posed whether this precedent is always appropriate, but it seems to be acceptable to the European Commission as it has appeared in several pieces of legislation implementing European law and has not been challenged.

Thus whilst on a first glance the obligations of distributors appear to be very much of a subsidiary nature to those of producers, it does not seem that there is really a dual standard operating. This is because of the flexible concept of the distributor's obligation to exercise due care, which in appropriate circumstances can be quite extensive. Equally, the obligations of producers are only those which are appropriate within the limits of their activities.

## New offences

Regulation 12 of the GPSR 1994 creates offences which punish producers who place an unsafe product on the market (breach of reg. 7) or distributors who in breach of reg. 9(a) supply products which they know, or should have presumed on the basis of information in their possession, are dangerous products. Regulation 13 also makes it an offence for any producer or distributor to offer or agree to place on the market any dangerous product, or to expose or possess such product for placing on the market, or to offer or agree to supply any dangerous product or expose or possess any such product for supply. A dangerous product is any product other than a safe product (reg. 2(1)). Regulation 13 therefore covers matters preparatory to the actual placing of the product on the market or its supply.

The way this set of offences has been drawn up is rather perplexing. Those created by reg. 12 seem to create a strict liability offence for producers but require at least constructive knowledge for a distributor to be liable. This is even more peculiar given that the reg. 13 offences, which involve preparatory acts, do not require a distributor to have knowledge in order to be liable. Thus a distributor can be strictly liable for possessing goods for supply, but is only liable for actually supplying them if he knew or ought to have known that they were dangerous.

It is also surprising that the GPSR 1994 impose liability for distributors failing to comply with only one of the two specific obligations placed on them by reg. 9. Indeed it is strange that an offence is based on this obligation as it is only part of the distributor's general obligation to take due care to help ensure compliance with the producer's obligation to market only safe products.

The offences defined in regs 12 and 13 are subject to the due diligence defence in reg. 14.

## Due diligence defence

In common with many regulatory offences in the consumer law field, reg. 14 of the GPSR 1994 provides for a due diligence defence. This provides a defence for a person who can show that he took all reasonable steps and exercised all due diligence to avoid committing the offence. There is a great deal of case law on the defence, too much to be considered in detail here: suffice it to note that some commentators suggest that 'reasonable precautions' involves 'setting up a system to ensure that things will not go wrong' and 'due diligence' means 'seeing that the system works properly'.

A person charged with an offence under the GPSR 1994 who alleges the commission of the offence was due to the act or default of another, or to reliance on information given by another, cannot rely on the defence, without leave of the court, unless a notice under reg. 14(3) is served seven days before the hearing of the proceedings on the person bringing the proceedings (reg. 14(2)). This notice must give such information identifying or assisting in the identification of the person committing the act or default as is in the possession of the person serving the notice at the time it is served (reg. 14(3)). In order for a defendant to claim the due diligence defence by alleging reliance on information supplied by another, the defendant must show that it was reasonable in all the circumstances to have relied on the information, having regard in particular to the steps taken, and those which might reasonably have been taken, by the defendant to verify the information and to whether he had any reason to disbelieve the information (reg. 14(4)).

Regulation 14(5) provides that the due diligence defences set out in reg. 14(1) and in the CPA 1987, s. 39(1), shall not apply where the defendant has contravened reg. 9(b), which requires distributors to participate in the monitoring of products by passing on information on product risks and cooperating to avoid those risks. Breach of reg. 9(b) is not of itself an offence, but a person who has not taken these steps cannot claim to have acted with due diligence if charged with breaching reg. 9(a) or an offence under reg. 13. In some ways this specific exclusion merely makes explicit what would no doubt have been the result if the defendant had tried to invoke the due diligence defence in such circumstances, but its value lies in the fact that a distributor cannot seek to blame non-compliance with obligations under reg. 9(b) on the actions of an employee. In fact the due diligence defence will only rarely need to be invoked by distributors because their criminal liability is not as strict as that of producers. They are only expected to act with due care and on the basis of what was known or should have been known to them and so in most cases, save where they try to blame one of their own employees, a defence to the general charge will be as easy to frame as the due diligence defence.

One of the major criticisms of the way the courts have interpreted the due diligence defence is that they have allowed companies to exonerate themselves by blaming employees. Thus in *Tesco Supermarkets Ltd* v *Nattrass* [1972] AC 153 the House of Lords held a store manager to be another person from the company and hence the company could use his actions as the basis for a due diligence defence. The obvious danger of this approach was spotted by Lord Widgery CJ in *McGuire* v *Sittingbourne Co-operative Society Ltd* [1976] Crim LR 268 who said:

> Unless some little care is taken in regard to these matters, we may find the administration of this Act sliding down to the sort of slipshod level at which all a defendant has to do is to say in general terms that the default must have been due to somebody in the shop, 'one of the girls', or some expression like that, and thereby satisfy the onus cast on him.

### Persons liable

The due diligence defence commonly runs in tandem with bypass provisions which allow the person who caused the offence to be committed by the original defendant to be prosecuted and such a provision is to be found in reg. 15(1) of the GPSR 1994. This provides that where the commission of the offence was due to the act or default of some other person in the course of a commercial activity of his the other person shall be guilty of an offence. The other person may be prosecuted even if the person who would have been guilty of the offence, but for the due diligence defence, is not prosecuted. The inclusion of the words 'of his' after the phrase 'in the course of a commercial activity' prevent an employee from being prosecuted under this provision since the commercial activity is not the employee's but the employer's (see *R* v *Warwickshire County Council, ex parte Johnson* [1993] AC 583).

Where the offence is committed by a sole trader or partnership those responsible for the business will be guilty of the offences created by the GPSR 1994. In many cases, however, a company will be the defendant. It may, however, be desirable to prosecute those persons who are in effect the *alter ego* of the company. To prevent these persons hiding from their responsibilities behind the corporate veil, reg. 15(2) provides that where a body corporate is guilty of an offence in respect of any act or default, which is shown to have been committed with the consent or connivance of, or which is attributable to any neglect on the part of, any director, manager, secretary or other similar officer of the body corporate or any person who was purporting to act in any such capacity, then that person as well as the body corporate shall be guilty of the offence.

## Enforcement

Regulation 11 of the GPSR 1994 extends the enforcement powers under the CPA 1987 to cover the provisions of the Regulations. Thus provisions in the CPA 1987 relating to prohibition notices, notices to warn, suspension notices and appeals therefrom, forfeiture and powers to obtain information are applied to products covered by the Regulations. In addition enforcement authorities with duties under the CPA 1987, the Medicines Act 1968 and food legislation are placed under similar duties to enforce the GPSR 1994.

## Penalties

Conviction of an offence under reg. 12 or reg. 13 will lead to imprisonment for up to three months and/or a fine not exceeding level 5 (reg. 17). The maximum prison sentence for contravening a prohibition notice, notice to warn or suspension notice is reduced from six to three months (reg.11(d)).

# Appendix 1

# Text of the Sale and Supply of Goods Act 1994

### 1994 CHAPTER 35

An Act to amend the law relating to the sale of goods; to make provision as to the terms to be implied in certain agreements for the transfer of property in or the hire of goods, in hire-purchase agreements and on the exchange of goods for trading stamps and as to the remedies for breach of the terms of such agreements; and for connected purposes.        [3rd November 1994]

Be it enacted by the Queen's most Excellent Majesty, by and with the advice and consent of the Lords Spiritual and Temporal, and Commons, in the present Parliament assembled, and by the authority of the same, as follows:—

*Provisions relating to the United Kingdom*

## 1. Implied term about quality

(1)   In section 14 of the Sale of Goods Act 1979 (implied terms about quality or fitness) for subsection (2) there is substituted—

'(2)   Where the seller sells goods in the course of a business, there is an implied term that the goods supplied under the contract are of satisfactory quality.

(2A)   For the purposes of this Act, goods are of satisfactory quality if they meet the standard that a reasonable person would regard as satisfactory, taking account of any description of the goods, the price (if relevant) and all the other relevant circumstances.

(2B)   For the purposes of this Act, the quality of goods includes their state and condition and the following (among others) are in appropriate cases aspects of the quality of goods—

(a)   fitness for all the purposes for which goods of the kind in question are commonly supplied,

(b)   appearance and finish,

(c)   freedom from minor defects,

(d)   safety, and

(e)   durability.

(2C)   The term implied by subsection (2) above does not extend to any matter making the quality of goods unsatisfactory—

(a)   which is specifically drawn to the buyer's attention before the contract is made,

(b)   where the buyer examines the goods before the contract is made, which that examination ought to reveal, or

(c)   in the case of a contract for sale by sample, which would have been apparent on a reasonable examination of the sample.

(2)   In section 15 of that Act (sale by sample) in subsection (2)(c) for 'rendering them unmerchantable' there is substituted 'making their quality unsatisfactory'.

## 2.   Acceptance of goods and opportunity to examine them

(1)   In section 35 of the Sale of Goods Act 1979 (acceptance) for the words from 'when he intimates' to '(2)' there is substituted—

'subject to subsection (2) below —

(a)   when he intimates to the seller that he has accepted them, or

(b)   when the goods have been delivered to him and he does any act in relation to them which is inconsistent with the ownership of the seller.

(2)   Where goods are delivered to the buyer, and he has not previously examined them, he is not deemed to have accepted them under subsection (1) above until he has had a reasonable opportunity of examining them for the purpose—

(a)   of ascertaining whether they are in conformity with the contract, and

(b)   in the case of a contract for sale by sample, of comparing the bulk with the sample.

(3)   Where the buyer deals as consumer or (in Scotland) the contract of sale is a consumer contract, the buyer cannot lose his right to rely on subsection (2) above by agreement, waiver or otherwise.

(4)   The buyer is also deemed to have accepted the goods when after the lapse of a reasonable time he retains the goods without intimating to the seller that he has rejected them.

(5)   The questions that are material in determining for the purposes of subsection (4) above whether a reasonable time has elapsed include

whether the buyer has had a reasonable opportunity of examining the goods for the purpose mentioned in subsection (2) above.

(6)    The buyer is not by virtue of this section deemed to have accepted the goods merely because—

(a)    he asks for, or agrees to, their repair by or under an arrangement with the seller, or

(b)    the goods are delivered to another under a sub-sale or other disposition.

(7)    Where the contract is for the sale of goods making one or more commercial units, a buyer accepting any goods included in a unit is deemed to have accepted all the goods making the unit; and in this subsection 'commercial unit' means a unit division of which would materially impair the value of the goods or the character of the unit.

(8)'.

(2)    In section 34 of that Act (buyer to have opportunity to examine goods)—

(a)    the words from the beginning to '(2)' are repealed; and

(b)    at the end of that section there is inserted 'and, in the case of a contract for sale by sample, of comparing the bulk with the sample.'

## 3.  Right of partial rejection

(1)    After section 35 of the Sale of Goods Act 1979 there is inserted the following section—

### '35A.  Right of partial rejection

(1)    If the buyer—

(a)    has the right to reject the goods by reason of a breach on the part of the seller that affects some or all of them, but

(b)    accepts some of the goods, including, where there are any goods unaffected by the breach, all such goods,

he does not by accepting them lose his right to reject the rest.

(2)    In the case of a buyer having the right to reject an instalment of goods, subsection (1) above applies as if references to the goods were references to the goods comprised in the instalment.

(3)    For the purposes of subsection (1) above, goods are affected by a breach if by reason of the breach they are not in conformity with the contract.

(4)    This section applies unless a contrary intention appears in, or is to be implied from, the contract.'

(2)    At the beginning of section 11(4) of that Act (effect of accepting goods) there is inserted 'Subject to section 35A below'.

(3)    Section 30(4) of that Act (rejection of goods not within contract description) is repealed.

*Provisions relating to England and Wales and Northern Ireland*

## 4. Modification of remedies in non-consumer cases

(1)   After section 15 of the Sale of Goods Act 1979 there is inserted the following—

'*Miscellaneous*

### 15A   Modification of remedies for breach of condition in non-consumer cases

(1)   Where in the case of a contract of sale—

(a)   the buyer would, apart from this subsection, have the right to reject goods by reason of a breach on the part of the seller of a term implied by section 13, 14 or 15 above, but

(b)   the breach is so slight that it would be unreasonable for him to reject them,

then, if the buyer does not deal as consumer, the breach is not to be treated as a breach of condition but may be treated as a breach of warranty.

(2)   This section applies unless a contrary intention appears in, or is to be implied from, the contract.

(3)   It is for the seller to show that a breach fell within subsection (1)(b) above.

(4)   This section does not apply to Scotland.'

(2)   In section 30 of that Act (delivery of shortfall or excess) after subsection (2) there is inserted—

'(2A)   A buyer who does not deal as consumer may not—

(a)   where the seller delivers a quantity of goods less than he contracted to sell, reject the goods under subsection 1 above, or

(b)   where the seller delivers a quantity of goods larger than he contracted to sell, reject the whole under subsection (2) above,

if the shortfall or, as the case may be, the excess is so slight that it would be unreasonable for him to do so.

(2B)   It is for the seller to show that a shortfall or excess fell within subsection (2A) above.

(2C)   Subsections (2A) and (2B) above do not apply to Scotland.'

*Provisions relating to Scotland*

## 5.   Remedies for breach of contract

(1)   After section 15A of the Sale of Goods Act 1979, which is inserted by section 4(1) above, there is inserted the following section—

**'15B.   Remedies for breach of contract as respects Scotland**

(1)   Where in a contract of sale the seller is in breach of any term of the contract (express or implied), the buyer shall be entitled—

    (a)   to claim damages, and

    (b)   if the breach is material, to reject any goods delivered under the contract and treat it as repudiated.

(2)   Where a contract of sale is a consumer contract, then, for the purposes of subsection (1)(b) above, breach by the seller of any term (express or implied)—

    (a)   as to the quality of the goods or their fitness for a purpose,

    (b)   if the goods are, or are to be, sold by description, that the goods will correspond with the description,

    (c)   if the goods are, or are to be, sold by reference to a sample, that the bulk will correspond with the sample in quality,

shall be deemed to be a material breach.

(3)   This section applies to Scotland only.'

(2)   In section 30 of that Act (delivery of shortfall or excess) before subsection (3) there is inserted—

'(2D)   Where the seller delivers a quantity of goods—

    (a)   less than he contracted to sell, the buyer shall not be entitled to reject the goods under subsection (1) above,

    (b)   larger than he contracted to sell, the buyer shall not be entitled to reject the whole under subsection (2) above,

unless the shortfall or excess is material.

(2E)   Subsection (2D) above applies to Scotland only.'

(3)   After section 53 of that Act there is inserted the following section—

**'53A.   Measure of damages as respects Scotland**

(1)   The measure of damages for the seller's breach of contract is the estimated loss directly and naturally resulting, in the ordinary course of events, from the breach.

(2)   Where the seller's breach consists of the delivery of goods which are not of the quality required by the contract and the buyer retains the goods, such loss as aforesaid is prima facie the difference between the value of the goods at the time of delivery to the buyer and the value they would have had if they had fulfilled the contract.

(3)   This section applies to Scotland only.'

## 6.   Provision equivalent to Part I of Supply of Goods and Services Act 1982

Schedule 1 to this Act shall have effect for the purpose of making provision equivalent to Part I of the Supply of Goods and Services Act 1982 for Scotland.

*General*

## 7. Amendments and repeals

(1)   Schedule 2 to this Act (which makes minor and consequential amendments of the Sale of Goods Act 1979 and the Uniform Laws on International Sales Act 1967, and makes amendments of enactments relating to the supply of goods corresponding to the amendments of that Act of 1979 made by this Act) shall have effect.

(2)   The enactments mentioned in Schedule 3 to this Act are repealed to the extent specified in column 3 of that Schedule.

## 8. Short title, commencement and extent

(1)   This Act may be cited as the Sale and Supply of Goods Act 1994.

(2)   This Act shall come into force at the end of the period of two months beginning with the day on which it is passed.

(3)   This Act has effect in relation to contracts of sale of goods, hire purchase agreements, contracts for the transfer of goods, contracts for the hire of goods and redemptions of trading stamps for goods (as the case may be) made after this Act comes into force.

(4)   This Act extends to Northern Ireland.

## SCHEDULES

### SCHEDULE 1    PROVISION EQUIVALENT TO PART I OF SUPPLY OF GOODS AND SERVICES ACT 1982
### FOR SCOTLAND                               Section 6

1.   After Part I of the Supply of Goods and Services Act 1982 there is inserted the following Part—

'PART 1A    SUPPLY OF GOODS AS RESPECTS SCOTLAND

*Contracts for the transfer of property in goods*

### 11A.   The contracts concerned

(1)   In this Act in its application to Scotland a "contract for the transfer of goods" means a contract under which one person transfers or agrees to transfer to another the property in goods, other than an excepted contract.

(2)   For the purposes of this section an excepted contract means any of the following—

(a)   a contract of sale of goods;

(b)   a hire-purchase agreement;

(c)   a contract under which the property in goods is (or is to be) transferred in exchange for trading stamps on their redemption;

(d) a transfer or agreement to transfer for which there is no consideration;

(e) a contract intended to operate by way of mortgage, pledge, charge or other security.

(3) For the purposes of this Act in its application to Scotland a contract is a contract for the transfer of goods whether or not services are also provided or to be provided under the contract, and (subject to subsection (2) above) whatever is the nature of the consideration for the transfer or agreement to transfer.

### 11B. Implied terms about title, etc.

(1) In a contract for the transfer of goods, other than one to which subsection (3) below applies, there is an implied term on the part of the transferor that in the case of a transfer of the property in the goods he has a right to transfer the property and in the case of an agreement to transfer the property in the goods he will have such a right at the time when the property is to be transferred.

(2) In a contract for the transfer of goods, other than one to which subsection (3) below applies, there is also an implied term that—

(a) the goods are free, and will remain free until the time when the property is to be transferred, from any charge or encumbrance not disclosed or known to the transferee before the contract is made, and

(b) the transferee will enjoy quiet possession of the goods except so far as it may be disturbed by the owner or other person entitled to the benefit or any charge or encumbrance so disclosed or known.

(3) This subsection applies to a contract for the transfer of goods in the case of which there appears from the contract or is to be inferred from its circumstances an intention that the transferor should transfer only such title as he or a third person may have.

(4) In a contract to which subsection (3) above applies there is an implied term that all charges or encumbrances known to the transferor and not known to the transferee have been disclosed to the transferee before the contract is made.

(5) In a contract to which subsection (3) above applies there is also an implied term that none of the following will disturb the transferee's quiet possession of the goods, namely—

(a) the transferor;

(b) in a case where the parties to the contract intend that the transferor should transfer only such title as a third person may have, that person;

(c) anyone claiming through or under the transferor or that third person otherwise than under a charge or encumbrance disclosed or known to the transferee before the contract is made.

(6) In section 21 of the 1977 Act after subsection (3) there is inserted the following subsection—

"(3A) Notwithstanding anything in the foregoing provisions of this section, any term of a contract which purports to exclude or restrict liability for breach of the obligations arising under section 11B of the Supply of Goods and Services Act 1982 (implied terms about title, freedom from encumbrances and quiet possession in certain contracts for the transfer of property in goods) shall be void."

### 11C. Implied terms where transfer is by description

(1) This section applies where, under a contract for the transfer of goods, the transferor transfers or agrees to transfer the property in the goods by description.

(2) In such a case there is an implied term that the goods will correspond with the description.

(3) If the transferor transfers or agrees to transfer the property in the goods by reference to a sample as well as by description it is not sufficient that the bulk of the goods corresponds with the sample if the goods do not also correspond with the description.

(4) A contract is not prevented from falling within subsection (1) above by reason only that, being exposed for supply, the goods are selected by the transferee.

### 11D. Implied terms about quality or fitness

(1) Except as provided by this section and section 11E below and subject to the provisions of any other enactment, there is no implied term about the quality or fitness for any particular purpose of goods supplied under a contract for the transfer of goods.

(2) Where, under such a contract, the transferor transfers the property in goods in the course of a business, there is an implied term that the goods supplied under the contract are of satisfactory quality.

(3) For the purposes of this section and section 11E below, goods are of satisfactory quality if they meet the standard that a reasonable person would regard as satisfactory, taking account of any description of the goods, the price (if relevant) and all the other relevant circumstances.

(4) The term implied by subsection (2) above does not extend to any matter making the quality of goods unsatisfactory—

(a) which is specifically drawn to the transferee's attention before the contract is made,

(b) where the transferee examines the goods before the contract is made, which that examination ought to reveal, or

(c)   where the property in the goods is, or is to be, transferred by reference to a sample, which would have been apparent on a reasonable examation of the sample.

(5)   Subsection (6) below applies where, under a contract for the transfer of goods, the transferor transfers the property in goods in the course of a business and the transferee, expressly or by implication, makes known—

(a)   to the transferor, or

(b)   where the consideration or part of the consideration for the transfer is a sum payable by instalments and the goods were previously sold by a credit-broker to the transferor, to that credit-broker,

any particular purpose for which the goods are being acquired.

(6)   In that case there is (subject to subsection (7) below) an implied term that the goods supplied under the contract are reasonably fit for the purpose, whether or not that is a purpose for which such goods are commonly supplied.

(7)   Subsection (6) above does not apply where the circumstances show that the transferee does not rely, or that it is unreasonable for him to rely, on the skill or judgment of the transferor or credit-broker.

(8)   An implied term about quality or fitness for a particular purpose may be annexed by usage to a contract for the transfer of goods.

(9)   The preceding provisions of this section apply to a transfer by a person who in the course of a business is acting as agent for another as they apply to a transfer by a principal in the course of a business, except where that other is not transferring in the course of a business and either the transferee knows that fact or reasonable steps are taken to bring it to the transferee's notice before the contract concerned is made.

### 11E.   Implied terms where transfer is by sample

(1)   This section applies where, under a contract for the transfer of goods, the transferor transfers or agrees to transfer the property in the goods by reference to a sample.

(2)   In such a case there is an implied term—

(a)   that the bulk will correspond with the sample in quality;

(b)   that the transferee will have a reasonable opportunity of comparing the bulk with the sample; and

(c)   that the goods will be free from any defect, making their quality unsatisfactory, which would not be apparent on reasonable examination of the sample.

(3)   For the purposes of this section a transferor transfers or agrees to transfer the property in goods by reference to a sample where there is an express or implied term to that effect in the contract concerned.

## 11F.  Remedies for breach of contract

(1)   Where in a contract for the transfer of goods a transferor is in breach of any term of the contract (express or implied), the other party to the contract (in this section referred to as "the transferee") shall be entitled—

(a)   to claim damages; and

(b)   if the breach is material, to reject any goods delivered under the contract and treat it as repudiated.

(2)   Where a contract for the transfer of goods is a consumer contract and the transferee is the consumer, then, for the purposes of subsection (1)(b) above, breach by the transferor of any term (express or implied)—

(a)   as to the quality of the goods or their fitness for a purpose;

(b)   if the goods are, or are to be, transferred by description, that the goods will correspond with the description;

(c)   if the goods are, or are to be, transferred by reference to a sample, that the bulk will correspond with the sample in quality,
shall be deemed to be a material breach.

(3)   In subsection (2) above, "consumer contract" has the same meaning as in section 25(1) of the 1977 Act; and for the purposes of that subsection the onus of proving that a contract is not to be regarded as a consumer contract shall lie on the transferor.

*Contracts for the hire of goods*

## 11G.  The contracts concerned

(1)   In this Act in its application to Scotland a "contract for the hire of goods" means a contract under which one person ("the supplier") hires or agrees to hire goods to another, other than an excepted contract.

(2)   For the purposes of this section, an excepted contract means any of the following—

(a)   a hire-purchase agreement;

(b)   a contract under which goods are (or are to be) hired in exchange for trading stamps on their redemption.

(3)   For the purposes of this Act in its application to Scotland a contract is a contract for the hire of goods whether or not services are also provided or to be provided under the contract, and (subject to subsection (2) above) whatever is the nature of the consideration for the hire or agreement to hire.

## 11H.  Implied terms about right to transfer possession etc.

(1)   In a contract for the hire of goods there is an implied term on the part of the supplier that—

(a) in the case of a hire, he has a right to transfer possession of the goods by way of hire for the period of the hire; and

(b) in the case of an agreement to hire, he will have such a right at the time of commencement of the period of the hire.

(2) In a contract for the hire of goods there is also an implied term that the person to whom the goods are hired will enjoy quiet possession of the goods for the period of the hire except so far as the possession may be disturbed by the owner or other person entitled to the benefit of any charge or encumbrance disclosed or known to the person to whom the goods are hired before the contract is made.

(3) The preceding provisions of this section do not affect the right of the supplier to repossess the goods under an express or implied term of the contract.

### 11I.  Implied terms where hire is by description

(1) This section applies where, under a contract for the hire of goods, the supplier hires or agrees to hire the goods by description.

(2) In such a case there is an implied term that the goods will correspond with the description.

(3) If under the contract the supplier hires or agrees to hire the goods by reference to a sample as well as by description it is not sufficient that the bulk of the goods corresponds with the sample if the goods do not also correspond with the description.

(4) A contract is not prevented from falling within subsection (1) above by reason only that, being exposed for supply, the goods are selected by the person to whom the goods are hired.

### 11J.  Implied terms about quality or fitness

(1) Except as provided by this section and section 11K below and subject to the provisions of any other enactment, there is no implied term about the quality or fitness for any particular purpose of goods hired under a contract for the hire of goods.

(2) Where, under such a contract, the supplier hires goods in the course of a business, there is an implied term that the goods supplied under the contract are of satisfactory quality.

(3) For the purposes of this section and section 11K below, goods are of satisfactory quality if they meet the standard that a reasonable person would regard as satisfactory, taking account of any description of the goods, the consideration for the hire (if relevant) and all the other relevant circumstances.

(4) The term implied by subsection (2) above does not extend to any matter making the quality of goods unsatisfactory—

(a)   which is specifically drawn to the attention of the person to whom the goods are hired before the contract is made, or

(b)   where that person examines the goods before the contract is made, which that examination ought to reveal; or

(c)   where the goods are hired by reference to a sample, which would have been apparent on reasonable examination of the sample.

(5)   Subsection (6) below applies where, under a contract for the hire of goods, the supplier hires goods in the course of a business and the person to whom the goods are hired, expressly or by implication, makes known—

(a)   to the supplier in the course of negotiations conducted by him in relation to the making of the contract; or

(b)   to a credit-broker in the course of negotiations conducted by that broker in relation to goods sold by him to the supplier before forming the subject matter of the contract,

any particular purpose for which the goods are being hired.

(6)   In that case there is (subject to subsection (7) below) an implied term that the goods supplied under the contract are reasonably fit for that purpose, whether or not that is a purpose for which such goods are commonly supplied.

(7)   Subsection (6) above does not apply where the circumstances show that the person to whom the goods are hired does not rely, or that it is unreasonable for him to rely, on the skill or judgment of the hirer or credit-broker.

(8)   An implied term about quality or fitness for a particular purpose may be annexed by usage to a contract for the hire of goods.

(9)   The preceding provisions of this section apply to a hire by a person who in the course of a business is acting as agent for another as they apply to a hire by a principal in the course of a business, except where that other is not hiring in the course of a business and either the person to whom the goods are hired knows that fact or reasonable steps are taken to bring it to that person's notice before the contract concerned is made.

**11K.   Implied terms where hire is by sample**

(1)   This section applies where, under a contract for the hire of goods, the supplier hires or agrees to hire the goods by reference to a sample.

(2)   In such a case there is an implied term—

(a)   that the bulk will correspond with the sample in quality; and

(b)   that the person to whom the goods are hired will have a reasonable opportunity of comparing the bulk with the sample; and

(c)   that the goods will be free from any defect, making their quality unsatisfactory, which would not be apparent on reasonable examination of the sample.

(3)   For the purposes of this section a supplier hires or agrees to hire goods by reference to a sample where there is an express or implied term to that effect in the contract concerned.

*Exclusion of implied terms, etc.*

**11L.   Exclusion of implied terms etc.**

(1)   Where a right, duty or liability would arise under a contract for the transfer of goods or a contract for the hire of goods by implication of law, it may (subject to subsection (2) below and the 1977 Act) be negatived or varied by express agreement, or by the course of dealing between the parties, or by such usage as binds both parties to the contract.

(2)   An express term does not negative a term implied by the preceding provisions of this Part of this Act unless inconsistent with it.

(3)   Nothing in the preceding provisions of this Part of this Act prejudices the operation of any other enactment or any rule of law whereby any term (other than one relating to quality or fitness) is to be implied in a contract for the transfer of goods or a contract for the hire of goods.'

2.   In section 18(1) of that Act—

(a)   in paragraph (b) of the definition of 'credit-brokerage' after 'bailment' there is inserted 'or as regards Scotland the hire';

(b)   in the definition of 'goods'—

(i)     for 'include all personal chattels (including' there is substituted 'includes all personal chattels, other than things in action and money, and as regards Scotland all corporeal moveables; and in particular "goods" includes';

(ii)    for 'or bailment' there is substituted 'bailment or hire';

(iii)   '), other than things in action and money' is omitted.

3.   In section 18(2) of that Act after 'assignment' there is inserted 'assignation'.

4.   In section 20(6) of that Act after 'Act' there is inserted 'except Part IA, which extends only to Scotland' and for 'but not' there is substituted 'and Parts I and II do not extend'.

### SCHEDULE 2   MINOR AND CONSEQUENTIAL
### AMENDMENTS                     Section 7.

*The Trading Stamps Act 1964 (c. 71)*

1.—(1)   Section 4 of the Trading Stamps Act 1964 (terms to be implied on redemption of trading stamps) is amended as follows.

(2)   In subsection (1)(a) and (b) for 'warranty' there is substituted 'term' and for subsection (1)(c) there is substituted—

'(c)   an implied term that the goods are of satisfactory quality.'

(3)   For subsection (2) and (3) there is substituted—

'(2)   For the purposes of paragraph (c) of subsection (1) of this section, goods are of satisfactory quality if they meet the standard that a reasonable person would regard as satisfactory, taking account of any description of the goods and all the other relevant circumstances.

(2A)   For the purposes of that paragraph, the quality of goods includes their state and condition and the following (among others) are in appropriate cases aspects of the quality of goods—

(a)   fitness for all the purposes for which goods of the kind in question are commonly supplied,

(b)   appearance and finish,

(c)   freedom from minor defects,

(d)   safety, and

(e)   durability.

(2B)   The term implied by that paragraph does not extend to any matter making the quality of goods unsatisfactory—

(a)   which is specifically drawn to the attention of the person obtaining the goods before or at the time of redemption, or

(b)   where that person examines the goods before or at the time of redemption, which that examination ought to reveal.

(3)   As regards England and Wales, the terms implied by subsection (1) of this section are warranties.'

*The Trading Stamps Act (Northern Ireland) 1965 (c. 6 (NI))*

2.—(1)   Section 4 of the Trading Stamps Act (Northern Ireland) 1965 (warranties to be implied on redemption of trading stamps) is amended as follows.

(2)   For subsection (1)(c) there is substituted—

'(c)   an implied warranty that the goods are of satisfactory quality.'

(3)   For subsection (2) there is substituted—

'(2)   For the purposes of paragraph (c) of subsection (1), goods are of satisfactory quality if they meet the standard that a reasonable person would regard as satisfactory, taking account of any description of the goods and all the other relevant circumstances.

(3)   For the purpose of that paragraph, the quality of goods includes their state and condition and the following (among others) are in appropriate cases aspects of the quality of goods—

(a)   fitness for all the purposes for which goods of the kind in question are commonly supplied,

(b)   appearance and finish,

(c)   freedom from minor defects,

(d)   safety, and

(e)   durability.

(4)   The warranty implied by that paragraph does not extend to any matter making the quality of goods unsatisfactory—

(a)   which is specifically drawn to the attention of the person obtaining the goods before or at the time of redemption, or

(b)   where that person examines the goods before or at the time of redemption, which that examination ought to reveal.'

*The Uniform Laws on International Sales Act 1967 (c. 45)*

3.   In section 1 of the Uniform Laws on International Sales Act 1967 (application of Uniform Law on the International Sale of Goods) in subsection (4)(c) for '12 to 15' there is substituted '12 to 15B'.

*The Supply of Goods (Implied Terms) Act 1973 (c. 13)*

4.—(1)   The Supply of Goods (Implied Terms) Act 1973 is amended as follows:

(2)   In section 8 (implied terms as to title)—

(a)   for 'condition' (in subsection (1)(a)) and for 'warranty' (in subsections (1)(b), (2)(a) and (2)(b)) there is substituted 'term'; and

(b)   at the end of that section there is inserted—

'(3)   As regards England and Wales and Northern Ireland, the term implied by subsection (1)(a) above is a condition and the terms implied by subsections (1)(b), (2)(a) and (2)(b) above are warranties.'

(3)   In section 9 (bailing or hiring by description)—

(a)   in subsection (1) for 'condition' there is substituted 'term'; and

(b)   after that subsection there is inserted—

'(1A)   As regards England and Wales and Northern Ireland, the term implied by subsection (1) above is a condition.'

(4)   In section 10 (implied undertakings as to quality or fitness)—

(a)   for subsection (2) there is substituted—

'(2)   Where the creditor bails or hires goods under a hire purchase agreement in the course of a business, there is an implied term that the goods supplied under the agreement are of satisfactory quality.

(2A)   For the purposes of this Act, goods are of satisfactory quality if they meet the standard that a reasonable person would regard as satisfactory, taking account of any description of the goods, the price (if relevant) and all the other relevant circumstances.

(2B)   For the purposes of this Act, the quality of goods includes their state and condition and the following (among others) are in appropriate cases aspects of the quality of goods—

(a)   fitness for all the purposes for which goods of the kind in question are commonly supplied,

(b)   appearance and finish,

(c)   freedom from minor defects,

(d)   safety, and

(e)   durability.

(2C)   The term implied by subsection (2) above does not extend to any matter making the quality of goods unsatisfactory—

(a)   which is specifically drawn to the attention of the person to whom the goods are bailed or hired before the agreement is made,

(b)   where that person examines the goods before the agreement is made, which that examination ought to reveal, or

(c)   where the goods are bailed or hired by reference to a sample, which would have been apparent on a reasonable examination of the sample';

(b)   for 'condition or warranty' (in subsections (1) and (4)) and for 'condition' (in subsection (3)) there is substituted 'term'; and

(c)   after subsection (6) there is inserted—

'(7)   As regards England and Wales and Northern Ireland, the terms implied by subsections (2) and (3) above are conditions.'

(5)   In section 11 (samples)—

(a)   at the beginning there is inserted '(1)';

(b)   for 'condition' there is substituted 'term';

(c)   in paragraph (c) for 'rendering them unmerchantable' there is substituted 'making their quality unsatisfactory'; and

(d)   at the end there is inserted—

'(2)   As regards England and Wales and Northern Ireland, the term implied by subsection (1) above is a condition.'

(6)   After that section there is inserted the following section—

**'11A.   Modification of remedies for breach of statutory condition in non-consumer cases**

(1)   Where in the case of a hire-purchase agreement—

(a)   the person to whom goods are bailed would, apart from this subsection, have the right to reject them by reason of a breach on the part of the creditor of a term implied by section 9, 10 or 11(1)(a) or (c) above, but

(b)   the breach is so slight that it would be unreasonable for him to reject them,

then, if the person to whom the goods are bailed does not deal as consumer, the breach is not to be treated as a breach of condition but may be treated as a breach of warranty.

(2)  This section applies unless a contrary intention appears in, or is to be implied from, the agreement.

(3)  It is for the creditor to show—

(a)  that a breach fell within subsection (1)(b) above, and

(b)  that the person to whom the goods were bailed did not deal as consumer.

(4)  The references in this section to dealing as consumer are to be construed in accordance with Part I of the Unfair Contract Terms Act 1977.

(5)  This section does not apply to Scotland.'

(7)  For section 12 (exclusion of implied terms and conditions) there is substituted the following section—

**'12.  Exclusion of implied terms**

An express term does not negative a term implied by this Act unless inconsistent with it.'

(8)  After section 12 there is inserted the following section—

**'12A.  Remedies for breach of hire-purchase agreement as respects Scotland**

(1)  Where in a hire-purchase agreement the creditor is in breach of any term of the agreement (express or implied), the person to whom the goods are hired shall be entitled—

(a)  to claim damages, and

(b)  if the breach is material, to reject any goods delivered under the agreement and treat it as repudiated.

(2)  Where a hire-purchase agreement is a consumer contract, then, for the purposes of subsection (1) above, breach by the creditor of any term (express or implied)—

(a)  as to the quality of the goods or their fitness for a purpose,

(b)  if the goods are, or are to be, hired by description, that the goods will correspond with the description,

(c)  if the goods are, or are to be, hired by reference to a sample, that the bulk will correspond with the sample in quality,
shall be deemed to be a material breach.

(3)  In subsection (2) above "consumer contract" has the same maaning as in section 25(1) of the Unfair Contract Terms Act 1977; and for the purposes of that subsection the onus of proving that a hire-purchase agreement is not to be regarded as a consumer contract shall lie on the creditor.

(4)  This section applies to Scotland only.'

(9)  In section 15 (supplementary)—

(a)  in subsection (1), from '"condition" and "warranty"' to 'material to the agreement' are omitted;

(b)   subsection (2) is omitted; and

(c)   in subsection (4), for 'condition or warranty' there is substituted 'term'.

### The Sale of Goods Act 1979 (c. 54)

5.—(1)   The Sale of Goods Act 1979 is amended as follows.

(2)   In section 11 (when condition to be treated as warranty)—

(a)   for subsection (1) there is substituted—

'(1)   This section does not apply to Scotland.'; and

(b)   subsection (5) is omitted.

(3)   In section 12 (implied terms about title etc.)—

(a)   for 'condition' (in subsection (1)) and for 'warranty' (in subsections (2), (4) and (5)) there is substituted 'term'; and

(b)   after subsection (5) there is inserted—

'(5A)   As regards England and Wales and Northern Ireland, the term implied by subsection (1) above is a condition and the terms implied by subsections (2), (4) and (5) above are warranties.'

(4)   In section 13 (sale by description)—

(a)   in subsection (1) for 'condition' there is substituted 'term'; and

(b)   after that subsection there is inserted—

'(1A)   As regards England and Wales and Northern Ireland, the term implied by subsection (1) above is a condition.'

(5)   In section 14 (implied terms about quality or fitness)—

(a)   for 'condition or warranty' (in subsections (1) and (4)) and for 'condition' (in subsection (3)) there is substituted 'term'; and

(b)   for subsection (6) there is substituted—

'(6)   As regards England and Wales and Northern Ireland, the terms implied by subsections (2) and (3) above are conditions.'

(6)   In section 15 (sale by sample)—

(a)   in subsection (2), for 'condition' there is substituted 'term' and paragraph (b) is omitted; and

(b)   for subsection (3) there is substituted—

'(3)   As regards England and Wales and Northern Ireland, the term implied by subsection (2) above is a condition.'

(7)   In section 53 (remedy for breach of warranty) for subsection (5) there is substituted—

'(5)   This section does not apply to Scotland.'

(8)   In section 55 (exclusion of implied terms) in subsection (2) for 'condition or warranty' (in both places) there is substituted 'term'.

(9)   In section 61 (interpretation)—

(a)   in subsection (1)—

(i)   after the definition of 'buyer' there is inserted—

' ''consumer contract'' has the same meaning as in section 25(1) of the Unfair Contract Terms Act 1977; and for the purposes of this Act the onus of proving that a contract is not to be regarded as a consumer contract shall lie on the seller'; and

(ii)   the definition of 'quality' is omitted;

(b)   subsection (2) is omitted; and

(c)   after subsection (5) there is inserted—

'(5A)   References in this Act to dealing as consumer are to be construed in accordance with Part I of the Unfair Contract Terms Act 1977; and, for the purposes of this Act, it is for a seller claiming that the buyer does not deal as consumer to show that he does not.'

(10)   For the heading *'Conditions and warranties'* that precedes sections 10 to 14 there is substituted the heading *'Implied terms etc.'*.

*The Supply of Goods and Services Act 1982 (c. 29)*

6.—(1)   The Supply of Goods and Services Act 1982 is amended as follows.

(2)   In section 1 (the contracts concerned), in subsections (1) and (3) after 'Act' there is inserted 'in its application to England and Wales and Northern Ireland'.

(3)   In section 4 (contracts for transfer: quality or fitness) for subsections (2) and (3) there is substituted—

'(2)   Where, under such a contract, the transferor transfers the property in goods in the course of a business, there is an implied condition that the goods supplied under the contract are of satisfactory quality.

(2A)   For the purposes of this section and section 5 below, goods are of satisfactory quality if they meet the standard that a reasonable person would regard as satisfactory, taking account of any description of the goods, the price (if relevant) and all the other relevant circumstances.

(3)   The condition implied by subsection (2) above does not extend to any matter making the quality of goods unsatisfactory—

(a)   which is specifically drawn to the transferee's attention before the contract is made,

(b)   where the transferee examines the goods before the contract is made, which that examination ought to reveal, or

(c)   where the property in the goods is transferred by reference to a sample, which would have been apparent on a reasonable examination of the sample.';

and subsection (9) is omitted.

(4)   In section 5 (transfer by sample)—

(a)  in subsection (2)(c), for 'rendering them unmerchantable' there is substituted 'making their quality unsatisfactory'; and

(b)  subsection (3) is omitted.

(5)  After section 5 there is inserted the following section—

'**5A.   Modification of remedies for breach of statutory condition in non-consumer cases**

5A.—(1)   Where in the case of a contract for the transfer of goods—

(a)  the transferee would, apart from this subsection, have the right to treat the contract as repudiated by reason of a breach on the part of the transferor of a term implied by section 3, 4 or 5(2)(a) or (c) above, but

(b)  the breach is so slight that it would be unreasonable for him to do so,

then, if the transferee does not deal as consumer, the breach is not to be treated as a breach of condition but may be treated as a breach of warranty.

(2)  This section applies unless a contrary intention appears in, or is to be implied from, the contract.

(3)  It is for the transferor to show that a breach fell within subsection (1)(b) above.'

(6)  In section 6 (the contracts concerned) in subsections (1) and (3) after 'Act' there is inserted 'in its application to England and Wales and Northern Ireland'.

(7)  In section 9 (contracts for hire: quality or fitness) for subsections (2) and (3) there is substituted—

'(2)  Where, under such a contract, the bailor bails goods in the course of a business, there is an implied condition that the goods supplied under the contract are of satisfactory quality.

(2A)  For the purposes of this section and section 10 below, goods are of satisfactory quality if they meet the standard that a reasonable person would regard as satisfactory, taking account of any description of the goods, the consideration for the bailment (if relevant) and all the other relevant circumstances.

(3)  The condition implied by subsection (2) above does not extend to any matter making the quality of goods unsatisfactory—

(a)  which is specifically drawn to the bailee's attention before the contract is made,

(b)  where the bailee examines the goods before the contract is made, which that examination ought to reveal, or

(c)  where the goods are bailed by reference to a sample, which would have been apparent on a reasonable examination of the sample.';

and subsection (9) is omitted.

(8)  In section 10 (hire by sample)—

(a)   in subsection (2)(c), for 'rendering them unmerchantable' there is substituted 'making their quality unsatisfactory'; and

(b)   subsection (3) is omitted.

(9)   After section 10 there is inserted the following section—

**'10A.   Modification of remedies for breach of statutory condition in non-consumer cases**

(1)   Where in the case of a contract for the hire of goods—

(a)   the bailee would, apart from this subsection, have the right to treat the contract as repudiated by reason of a breach on the part of the bailor of a term implied by section 8, 9 or 10(2)(a) or (c) above, but

(b)   the breach is so slight that it would be unreasonable for him to do so,

then, if the bailee does not deal as consumer, the breach is not to be treated as a breach of condition but may be treated as a breach of warranty.

(2)   This section applies unless a contrary intention appears in, or is to be implied from, the contract.

(3)   It is for the bailor to show that a breach fell within subsection (1)(b) above.'

(10)   In section 18 (interpretation) in subsection (1) the definition of 'quality' is omitted and at the end of that section there is inserted—

'(3)   For the purposes of this Act, the quality of goods includes their state and condition and the following (among others) are in appropriate cases aspects of the quality of goods—

(a)   fitness for all the purposes for which goods of the kind in question are commonly supplied,

(b)   appearance and finish,

(c)   freedom from minor defects,

(d)   safety, and

(e)   durability.

(4)   References in this Act to dealing as consumer are to be construed in acordance with Part I of the Unfair Contract Terms Act 1977; and, for the purposes of this Act, it is for the transferor or bailor claiming that the transferee or bailee does not deal as consumer to show that he does not.'

## SCHEDULE 3   REPEALS     Section 7.

| Chapter | Short title | Extent of repeal |
|---|---|---|
| 1973 c. 13 | The Supply of Goods (Implied Terms) Act 1973. | In section 15, in subsection (1), the words from ' "condition" and "warranty" ' to 'material to the agreement' and subsection (2). |
| 1979 c. 54. | The Sale of Goods Act 1979. | Section 11(5). Section 15(2)(b). Section 30(4). In section 34, the words from the beginning to '(2)'. In section 61, in subsection (1) the definition of 'quality' and subsection (2). |
| 1982 c. 29. | The Supply of Goods and Services Act 1982. | Section 4(9). Section 5(3). Section 9(9). Section 10(3). Section 17(1). In section 18(1), the definition of "quality" and in the definition of 'goods' the words '), other than things in action and money'. |

# Appendix 2

---

## Text of Key Legislative Provisions in Amended Form

**Sale of Goods Act 1979, sections 14, 15, 15A, 30, 34, 35 and 35A**

### 14. Implied terms about quality or fitness

(1)  Except as provided by this section and section 15 below and subject to any other enactment, there is no implied term about the quality or fitness for any particular purpose of goods supplied under a contract of sale.

(2)  Where the seller sells goods in the course of a business, there is an implied term that the goods supplied under the contract are of satisfactory quality.

(2A)  For the purposes of this Act, goods are of satisfactory quality if they meet the standard that a reasonable person would regard as satisfactory, taking account of any description of the goods, the price (if relevant) and all the other relevant circumstances.

(2B)  For the purposes of this Act, the quality of goods includes their state and condition and the following (among others) are in appropriate cases aspects of the quality of goods—

(a)  fitness for all the purposes for which goods of the kind in question are commonly supplied,

(b)  appearance and finish,

(c)  freedom from minor defects,

(d)  safety, and

(e)  durability.

(2C)  The term implied by subsection (2) above does not extend to any matter making the quality of goods unsatisfactory—

(a)  which is specifically drawn to the buyer's attention before the contract is made,

(b)  where the buyer examines the goods before the contract is made, which that examination ought to reveal, or

(c)  in the case of a contract for sale by sample, which would have been apparent on a reasonable examination of the sample.

(3)  Where the seller sells goods in the course of a business and the buyer, expressly or by implication, makes known—

(a)  to the seller, or

(b)  where the purchase price or part of it is payable by instalments and the goods were previously sold by a credit-broker to the seller, to that credit-broker,

any particular purpose for which the goods are being bought, there is an implied term that the goods supplied under the contract are reasonably fit for that purpose, whether or not that is a purpose for which such goods are commonly supplied, except where the circumstances show that the buyer does not rely, or that it is unreasonable for him to rely, on the skill or judgment of the seller or credit-broker.

(4)  An implied term about quality or fitness for a particular purpose may be annexed to a contract of sale by usage.

(5)  The preceding provisions of this section apply to a sale by a person who in the course of a business is acting as agent for another as they apply to a sale by a principal in the course of a business, except where that other is not selling in the course of a business and either the buyer knows that fact or reasonable steps are taken to bring it to the notice of the buyer before the contract is made.

(6)  As regards England and Wales and Northern Ireland, the terms implied by subsections (2) and (3) above are conditions.

(7)  Paragraph 5 of Schedule 1 below applies in relation to a contract made on or after 18 May 1973 and before the appointed day,* and paragraph 6 in relation to one made before 18 May 1973.

(8)  In subsection (7) above and paragraph 5 of Schedule 1 below references to the appointed day are to the day appointed for the purposes of those provisions by an order of the Secretary of State made by statutory instrument.

*19 May 1985 (SI 1983/1572).

### 15.  Sale by sample

(1)  A contract of sale is a contract for sale by sample where there is an express or implied term to that effect in the contract.

(2)  In the case of a contract for sale by sample there is an implied condition—

(a)  that the bulk will correspond with the sample in quality;

[(b)  repealed]

(c)  that the goods will be free from any defect, making their quality unsatisfactory, which would not be apparent on reasonable examination of the sample.

(3)  As regards England and Wales and Northern Ireland, the term implied by subsection (2) above is a condition.

(4)  Paragraph 7 of Schedule 1 below applies in relation to a contract made before 18 May 1973.

### 15A.  Modification of remedies for breach of condition in non-consumer cases

(1)  Where in the case of a contract of sale—

(a)  the buyer would, apart from this subsection, have the right to reject goods by reason of a breach on the part of the seller of a term implied by section 13, 14 or 15 above, but

(b)  the breach is so slight that it would be unreasonable for him to reject them,

then, if the buyer does not deal as consumer, the breach is not to be treated as a breach of condition but may be treated as a breach of warranty.

(2)  This section applies unless a contrary intention appears in, or is to be implied from, the contract.

(3)  It is for the seller to show that a breach fell within subsection (1)(b) above.

(4)  This section does not apply to Scotland.

### 30.  Delivery of wrong quantity

(1)  Where the seller delivers to the buyer a quantity of goods less than he contracted to sell, the buyer may reject them, but if the buyer accepts the goods so delivered he must pay for them at the contract rate.

(2)  Where the seller delivers to the buyer a quantity of goods larger than he contracted to sell, the buyer may accept the goods included in the contract and reject the rest, or he may reject the whole.

(2A)  A buyer who does not deal as consumer may not—

(a)  where the seller delivers a quantity of goods less than he contracted to sell, reject the goods under subsection (1) above, or

(b)  where the seller delivers a quantity of goods larger than he contracted to sell, reject the whole under subsection (2) above,

if the shortfall or, as the case may be, excess is so slight that it would be unreasonable for him to do so.

(2B)  It is for the seller to show that a shortfall or excess fell within subsection (2A) above.

(2C)   Subsections (2A) and (2B) above do not apply to Scotland.

(2D)   Where the seller delivers a quantity of goods—

(a)   less than he contracted to sell, the buyer shall not be entitled to reject the goods under subsection (1) above,

(b)   larger than he contracted to sell, the buyer shall not be entitled to reject the whole under subsection (2) above,

unless the shortfall or excess is material.

(2E)   Subsection (2D) above applies to Scotland only.

(3)   Where the seller delivers to the buyer a quantity of goods larger than he contracted to sell and the buyer accepts the whole of the goods so delivered he must pay for them at the contract rate.

[(4)   Repealed.]

(5)   This section is subject to any usage of trade, special agreement, or course of dealing between the parties.

## 34.   Buyer's right of examining the goods

Unless otherwise agreed, when the seller tenders delivery of goods to the buyer, he is bound on request to afford the buyer a reasonable opportunity of examining the goods for the purpose of ascertaining whether they are in conformity with the contract and, in the case of a contract for sale by sample, of comparing the bulk with the sample.

## 35.   Acceptance

(1)   The buyer is deemed to have acepted the goods subject to subsection (2) below—

(a)   when he intimates to the seller that he has accepted them, or

(b)   when the goods have been delivered to him and he does any act in relation to them which is inconsistent with the ownership of the seller.

(2)   Where goods are delivered to the buyer, and he has not previously examined them, he is not deemed to have accepted them under subsection (1) above until he has had a reasonable opportunity of examining them for the purpose—

(a)   of ascertaining whether they are in conformity with the contract, and

(b)   in the case of a contract for sale by sample, of comparing the bulk with the sample.

(3)   Where the buyer deals as consumer or (in Scotland) the contract of sale is a consumer contract, the buyer cannot lose his right to rely on subsection (2) above by agreement, waiver or otherwise.

(4)   The buyer is also deemed to have accepted the goods when after the lapse of a reasonable time he retains the goods without intimating to the seller that he has rejected them.

(5)   The questions that are material in determining for the purposes of subsection (4) above whether a reasonable time has elapsed include whether the buyer has had a reasonable opportunity of examining the goods for the purpose mentioned in subsection (2) above.

(6)   The buyer is not by virtue of this section deemed to have accepted the goods merely because—

(a)   he asks for, or agrees to, their repair by or under an arrangement with the seller, or

(b)   the goods are delivered to another under a sub-sale or other disposition.

(7)   Where the contract is for the sale of goods making one or more commercial units, a buyer accepting any goods included in a unit is deemed to have accepted all the goods making the unit; and in this subsection 'commercial unit' means a unit division of which would materially impair the value of the goods or the character of the unit.

(8)   Paragraph 10 of Schedule 1 below applies in relation to a contract made before 22 April 1967 or (in the application of this Act to Northern Ireland) 28 July 1967.

### 35A.   Right of partial rejection

(1)   If the buyer

(a)   has the right to reject the goods by reason of a breach on the part of the seller that affects some or all of them, but

(b)   accepts some of the goods, including, where there are any goods unaffected by the breach, all such goods,

he does not by accepting them lose his right to reject the rest.

(2)   In the case of a buyer having the right to reject an instalment of goods, subsection (1) above applies as if references to the goods were references to the goods comprised in the instalment.

(3)   For the purposes of subsection (1) above, goods are affected by a breach if by reason of the breach they are not in conformity with the contract.

(4)   This section applies unless a contrary intention appears in, or is to be implied from, the contract.

### Supply of Goods (Implied Terms) Act 1973, section 10, 11 and 11A

### 10.   Implied undertakings as to quality or fitness

(1)   Except as provided by this section and section 11 below and subject to the provisions of any other enactment, including any enactment of the Parliament of Northern Ireland or the Northern Ireland Assembly, there is no implied term as to the quality or fitness for any particular purpose of goods bailed or (in Scotland) hired under a hire-purchase agreement.

(2) Where the creditor bails or hires goods under a hire purchase agreement in the course of a business, there is an implied term that the goods supplied under the agreement are of satisfactory quality.

(2A) For the purposes of this Act, goods are of satisfactory quality if they meet the standard that a reasonable person would regard as satisfactory, taking account of any description of the goods, the price (if relevant) and all the other relevant circumstances.

(2B) For the purposes of this Act, the quality of goods includes their state and condition and the following (among others) are in appropriate cases aspects of the quality of goods—

(a) fitness for all the purposes for which goods of the kind in question are commonly supplied,

(b) appearance and finish,

(c) freedom from minor defects,

(d) safety, and

(e) durability.

(2C) The term implied by subsection (2) above does not extend to any matter making the quality of goods unsatisfactory—

(a) which is specifically drawn to the attention of the person to whom the goods are bailed or hired before the agreement is made,

(b) where that person examines the goods before the agreement is made, which that examination ought to reveal, or

(c) where the goods are bailed or hired by reference to a sample, which would have been apparent on a reasonable examination of the sample.

(3) Where the creditor bails or hires goods under a hire-purchase agreement in the course of a business and the person to whom the goods are bailed or hired, expressly or by implication, makes known—

(a) to the creditor in the course of negotiations conducted by the creditor in relation to the making of the hire-purchase agreement, or

(b) to a credit-broker in the course of negotiations conducted by that broker in relation to goods sold by him to the creditor before forming the subject matter of the hire-purchase agreement,

any particular purpose for which the goods are being bailed or hired, there is an implied term that the goods supplied under the agreement are reasonably fit for that purpose, whether or not that is a purpose for which such goods are commonly supplied, except where the circumstances show that the person to whom the goods are bailed or hired does not rely, or that it is unreasonable for him to rely, on the skill or judgment of the creditor or credit-broker.

(4) An implied term as to quality or fitness for a particular purpose may be annexed to a hire-purchase agreement by usage.

(5)   The preceding provisions of this section apply to a hire-purchase agreement made by a person who in the course of a business is acting as agent for the creditor as they apply to an agreement made by the creditor in the course of a business, except where the creditor is not bailing or hiring in the course of a business and either the person to whom the goods are bailed or hired knows that fact or reasonable steps are taken to bring it to the notice of that person before the agreement is made.

(6)   In subsection (3) above and this subsection—

(a)   'credit-broker' means a person acting in the course of a business of credit brokerage;

(b)   'credit brokerage' means the effecting of introductions of individuals desiring to obtain credit—

(i)    to persons carrying on any business so far as it relates to the provision of credit, or

(ii)   to other persons engaged in credit brokerage.

(7)   As regards England and Wales and Northern Ireland, the terms implied by subsections (2) and (3) above are conditions.

## 11.  Samples

(1)   Where under a hire-purchase agreement goods are bailed or (in Scotland) hired by reference to a sample, there is an implied term—

(a)   that the bulk will correspond with the sample in quality; and

(b)   that the person to whom the goods are bailed or hired will have a reasonable opportunity of comparing the bulk with the sample; and

(c)   that the goods will be free from any defect, making their quality unsatisfactory, which would not be apparent on reasonable examination of the sample.

(2)   As regards England and Wales and Northern Ireland, the term implied by subsection (1) above is a condition.

## 11A.  Modification of remedies for breach of statutory condition in non-consumer cases

(1)   Where in the case of a hire-purchase agreement—

(a)   the person to whom goods are bailed would, apart from this subsection, have the right to reject them by reason of a breach on the part of the creditor of a term implied by section 9, 10 or 11(1)(a) or (c) above, but

(b)   the breach is so slight that it would be unreasonable for him to reject them,

then, if the person to whom the goods are bailed does not deal as consumer, the breach is not to be treated as a breach of condition but may be treated as a breach of warranty.

(2) This section applies unless a contrary intention appears in, or is to be implied from, the agreement.

(3) It is for the creditor to show—

(a) that a breach fell within subsection (1)(b) above, and

(b) that the person to whom the goods were bailed did not deal as consumer.

(4) The references in this section to dealing as consumer are to be construed in accordance with Part I of the Unfair Contract Terms Act 1977.

(5) This section does not apply to Scotland.

**Supply of Goods and Services Act 1982, sections 4, 5, 5A, 9, 10 and 10A**

**4. Implied terms about quality or fitness**

(1) Except as provided by this section and section 5 below and subject to the provisions of any other enactment, there is no implied condition or warranty about the quality or fitness for any particular purpose of goods supplied under a contract for the transfer of goods.

(2) Where, under such a contract, the transferor transfers the property in goods in the course of a business, there is an implied condition that the goods supplied under the contract are of satisfactory quality.

(2A) For the purposes of this section and section 5 below, goods are of satisfactory quality if they meet the standard that a reasonable person would regard as satisfactory, taking account of any description of the goods, the price (if relevant) and all the other relevant circumstances.

(3) The condition implied by subsection (2) above does not extend to any matter making the quality of goods unsatisfactory—

(a) which is specifically drawn to the transferee's attention before the contract is made,

(b) where the transferee examines the goods before the contract is made, which that examination ought to reveal, or

(c) where the property in the goods is transferred by reference to a sample, which would have been apparent on a reasonable examination of the sample.

(4) Subsection (5) below applies where, under a contract for the transfer of goods, the transferor transfers the property in goods in the course of a business and the transferee, expressly or by implication, makes known—

(a) to the transferor, or

(b) where the consideration or part of the consideration for the transfer is a sum payable by instalments and the goods were previously sold by a credit-broker to the transferor, to that credit-broker,

any particular purpose for which the goods are being acquired.

(5) In that case there is (subject to subsection (6) below) an implied condition that the goods supplied under the contract are reasonably fit for that purpose, whether or not that is a purpose for which such goods are commonly supplied.

(6) Subsection (5) above does not apply where the circumstances show that the transferee does not rely, or that it is unreasonable for him to rely, on the skill or judgment of the transferor or credit-broker.

(7) An implied condition or warranty about quality or fitness for a particular purpose may be annexed by usage to a contract for the transfer of goods.

(8) The preceding provisions of this section apply to a transfer by a person who in the course of a business is acting as agent for another as they apply to a transfer by a principal in the course of a business, except where that other is not transferring in the course of a business and either the transferee knows that fact or reasonable steps are taken to bring it to the transferee's notice before the contract concerned is made.

**5. Implied terms where transfer is by sample**

(1) This section applies where, under a contract for the transfer of goods, the transferor transfers or agrees to transfer the property in the goods by reference to a sample.

(2) In such a case there is an implied condition—

(a) that the bulk will correspond with the sample in quality; and

(b) that the transferee will have a reasonable opportunity of comparing the bulk with the sample; and

(c) that the goods will be free from any defect, making their quality unsatisfactory, which would not be apparent on reasonable examination of the sample.

[(3) Repealed.]

(4) For the purposes of this section a transferor transfers or agrees to transfer the property in goods by reference to a sample where there is an express or implied term to that effect in the contract concerned.

**5A. Modification of remedies for breach of statutory condition in non-consumer cases**

(1) Where in the case of a contract for the transfer of goods—

(a) the transferee would, apart from this subsection, have the right to treat the contract as repudiated by reason of a breach on the part of the transferor of a term implied by section 3, 4 or 5(2)(a) or (c) above, but

(b) the breach is so slight that it would be unreasonable for him to do so,

then, if the transferee does not deal as consumer, the breach is not to be treated as a breach of condition but may be treated as a breach of warranty.

(2)  This section applies unless a contrary intention appears in, or is to be implied from, the contract.

(3)  It is for the transferor to show that a breach fell within subsection (1)(b) above.

## 9.  Implied terms about quality or fitness

(1)  Except as provided by this section and section 10 below and subject to the provisions of any other enactment, there is no implied condition or warranty about the quality or fitness for any particular purpose of goods bailed under a contract for the hire of goods.

(2)  Where, under such a contract, the bailor bails goods in the course of a business, there is an implied condition that the goods supplied under the contract are of satisfactory quality.

(2A)  For the purposes of this section and section 10 below, goods are of satisfactory quality if they meet the standard that a reasonable person would regard as satisfactory, taking account of any description of the goods, the consideration for the bailment (if relevant) and all the other relevant circumstances.

(3)  The condition implied by subsection (2) above does not extend to any matter making the quality of goods unsatisfactory—

(a)  which is specifically drawn to the bailee's attention before the contract is made,

(b)  where the bailee examines the goods before the contract is made, which that examination ought to reveal, or

(c)  where the goods are bailed by reference to a sample, which would have been apparent on a reasonable examination of the sample.

(4)  Subsection (5) below applies where, under a contract for the hire of goods, the bailor bails goods in the course of a business and the bailee, expressly or by implication, makes known—

(a)  to the bailor in the course of negotiations conducted by him in relation to the making of the contract, or

(b)  to a credit-broker in the course of negotiations conducted by that broker in relation to goods sold by him to the bailor before forming the subject matter of the contract,
any particular purpose for which the goods are being bailed.

(5)  In that case there is (subject to subsection (6) below) an implied condition that the goods supplied under the contract are reasonably fit for that purpose, whether or not that is a purpose for which such goods are commonly supplied.

(6)  Subsection (5) above does not apply where the circumstances show that the bailee does not rely, or that it is unreasonable for him to rely, on the skill or judgment of the bailor or credit-broker.

(7)   An implied condition or warranty about quality or fitness for a particular purpose may be annexed by usage to a contract for the hire of goods.

(8)   The preceding provisions of this section apply to a bailment by a person who in the course of a business is acting as agent for another as they apply to a bailment by a principal in the course of a business, except where that other is not bailing in the course of a business and either the bailee knows that fact or reasonable steps are taken to bring it to the bailee's notice before the contract concerned is made.

**10.   Implied terms where hire is by sample**

(1)   This section applies where, under a contract for the hire of goods, the bailor bails or agrees to bail the goods by reference to a sample.

(2)   In such a case there is an implied condition—

(a)   that the bulk will correspond with the sample in quality; and

(b)   that the bailee will have a reasonable opportunity of comparing the bulk with the sample; and

(c)   that the goods will be free from any defect, making their quality unsatisfactory, which would not be apparent on reasonable examination of the sample.

[(3)   Repealed.]

(4)   For the purposes of this section a bailor bails or agrees to bail goods by reference to a sample where there is an express or implied term to that effect in the contract concerned.

**10A.   Modification of remedies for breach of statutory condition in non-consumer cases**

(1)   Where in the case of a contract for the hire of goods—

(a)   the bailee would, apart from this subsection, have the right to treat the contract as repudiated by reason of a breach on the part of the bailor of a term implied by section 8, 9, 10(2)(a) or (c) above, but

(b)   the breach is so slight that it would be unreasonable for him to do so,

then, if the bailee does not deal as consumer, the breach is not to be treated as a breach of condition but may be treated as a breach of warranty.

(2)   This section applies unless a contrary intention appears in, or is to be implied from, the contract.

(3)   It is for the bailor to show that a breach fell within subsection (1)(b) above.

# Appendix 3

# Text of the Sale of Goods (Amendment) Act 1994

## 1994 CHAPTER 32

An Act to abolish the rule of law relating to the sale of goods in market overt.

[3rd November 1994]

Be it enacted by the Queen's most Excellent Majesty, by and with the advice and consent of the Lords Spiritual and Temporal, and Commons, in this present Parliament assembled, and by the authority of the same, as follows:—

**1. Repeal of s. 22(1) of the Sale of Goods Act 1979**

Section 22(1) (relating to the sale of goods in market overt) of the Sale of Goods Act 1979 is hereby repealed.

**2. Consequential repeals**

(1) Section 47 of the Laws in Wales Act 1542 (sale of stolen goods in a fair or market in Wales) is hereby repealed.

(2) In section 7(3) of the Sea Fisheries (Shellfish) Act 1967 (protection of fisheries for shellfish), the words 'sold in market overt or' shall be omitted.

**3. Short title, commencement and extent**

(1) This Act may be cited as the Sale of Goods (Amendment) Act 1994.

(2) This Act shall apply to any contract for sale of goods which is made after this Act comes into force.

(3) This Act shall come into force at the end of the period of two months beginning with the day on which it is passed.

(4) Section 1 and this section extend to Northern Ireland.

Appendix 4

---

# Text of the Unfair Terms in Consumer Contracts Regulations 1994

### SI 1994/3159

| | |
|---|---|
| *Made* | *8th December 1994* |
| *Laid before Parliament* | *14th December 1994* |
| *Coming into force* | *1st July 1995* |

Whereas the Secretary of State is a Minister designated[1] for the purposes of section 2(2) of the European Communities Act 1972 in relation to measures relating to consumer protection;

Now, the Secretary of State, in exercise of the powers conferred upon him by section 2(2) of that Act and of all other powers enabling him in that behalf hereby makes the following Regulations:—

**Citation and commencement**

**1.** These Regulations may be cited as the Unfair Terms in Consumer Contracts Regulations 1994 and shall come into force on 1st July 1995.

**Interpretation**

**2.**—(1) In these Regulations—

'business' includes a trade or profession and the activities of any government department or local or public authority;

'the Community' means the European Economic Community and the other States in the European Economic Area;

---

[1] SI 1993/2261.

'consumer' means a natural person who, in making a contract to which these Regulations apply, is acting for purposes which are outside his business;

'court' in relation to England and Wales and Northern Ireland means the High Court, and in relation to Scotland, the Court of Session;

'Director' means the Director General of Fair Trading;

'EEA Agreement' means the Agreement on the European Economic Area signed at Oporto on 2 May 1992 as adjusted by the protocol signed at Brussels on 17 March 1993;[2]

'member State' shall mean a State which is a contracting party to the EEA Agreement but until the EEA Agreement comes into force in relation to Liechtenstein does not include the State of Liechtenstein;

'seller' means a person who sells goods and who, in making a contract to which these Regulations apply, is acting for purposes relating to his business; and

'supplier' means a person who supplies goods or services and who, in making a contract to which these Regulations apply, is acting for purposes relating to his business.

(2)   In the application of these Regulations to Scotland for references to an 'injunction' or an 'interlocutory injunction' there shall be substituted references to an 'interdict' or 'interim interdict' respectively.

## Terms to which these Regulations apply

3.—(1)   Subject to the provisions of Schedule 1, these Regulations apply to any term in a contract concluded between a seller or supplier and a consumer where the said term has not been individually negotiated.

(2)   In so far as it is in plain, intelligible language, no assessment shall be made of the fairness of any term which—

(a)   defines the main subject-matter of the contract, or

(b)   concerns the adequacy of the price or remuneration, as against the goods or services sold or supplied.

(3)   For the purposes of these Regulations, a term shall always be regarded as not having been individually negotiated where it has been drafted in advance and the consumer has not been able to influence the substance of the term.

(4)   Notwithstanding that a specific term or certain aspects of it in a contract has been individually negotiated, these Regulations shall apply to the rest of a contract if an overall assessment of the contract indicates that it is a pre-formulated standard contract.

---

[2] Protocol 47 and certain Annexes to the EEA Agreement were amended by Decision No. 7/94 of the EEA Joint Committee which came into force on 1 July 1994 (OJ No. L 160, 28.6.1994, p. 1). Council Directive 93/13/EEC was added to Annex XIX to the Agreement by Annex 17 to the said Decision No. 7/94.

(5) It shall be for any seller or supplier who claims that a term was individually negotiated to show that it was.

## Unfair terms

**4.**—(1) In these Regulations, subject to paragraphs (2) and (3) below, 'unfair term' means any term which contrary to the requirement of good faith causes a significant imbalance in the parties' rights and obligations under the contract to the detriment of the consumer.

(2) An assessment of the unfair nature of a term shall be made taking into account the nature of the goods or services for which the contract was concluded and referring, as at the time of the conclusion of the contract, to all circumstances attending the conclusion of the contract and to all the other terms of the contract or of another contract on which it is dependent.

(3) In determining whether a term satisfies the requirement of good faith, regard shall be had in particular to the matters specified in Schedule 2 to these Regulations.

(4) Schedule 3 to these Regulations contains an indicative and non-exhaustive list of the terms which may be regarded as unfair.

## Consequence of inclusion of unfair terms in contracts

**5.**—(1) An unfair term in a contract concluded with a consumer by a seller or supplier shall not be binding on the consumer.

(2) The contract shall continue to bind the parties if it is capable of continuing in existence without the unfair term.

## Construction of written contracts

**6.** A seller or supplier shall ensure that any written term of a contract is expressed in plain, intelligible language, and if there is doubt about the meaning of a written term, the interpretation most favourable to the consumer shall prevail.

## Choice of law clauses

**7.** These Regulations shall apply notwithstanding any contract term which applies or purports to apply the law of a non-member State, if the contract has a close connection with the territory of the member States.

## Prevention of continued use of unfair terms

**8.**—(1) It shall be the duty of the Director to consider any complaint made to him that any contract term drawn up for general use is unfair, unless the complaint appears to the Director to be frivolous or vexatious.

(2) If having considered a complaint about any contract term pursuant to paragraph (1) above the Director considers that the contract term is unfair he may, if he considers it appropriate to do so, bring proceedings for an injunction (in which proceedings he may also apply for an interlocutory

injunction) against any person appearing to him to be using or recommending use of such a term in contracts concluded with consumers.

(3)   The Director may, if he considers it appropriate to do so, have regard to any undertakings given to him by or on behalf of any person as to the continued use of such a term in contracts concluded with consumers.

(4)   The Director shall give reasons for his decision to apply or not to apply, as the case may be, for an injunction in relation to any complaint which these Regulations require him to consider.

(5)   The court on an application by the Director may grant an injunction on such terms as it thinks fit.

(6)   An injunction may relate not only to use of a particular contract term drawn up for general use but to any similar term, or a term having like effect, used or recommended for use by any party to the proceedings.

(7)   The Director may arrange for the dissemination in such form and manner as he considers appropriate of such information and advice concerning the operation of these Regulations as may appear to him to be expedient to give to the public and to all persons likely to be affected by these Regulations.

*Ferrers*
Minister of State,
8th December 1994                    Department of Trade and Industry

### SCHEDULE 1    CONTRACTS AND PARTICULAR TERMS EXCLUDED FROM THE SCOPE OF THESE REGULATIONS          Regulation 3(1).

These Regulations do not apply to—
   (a)   any contract relating to employment;
   (b)   any contract relating to succession rights;
   (c)   any contract relating to rights under family law;
   (d)   any contract relating to the incorporation and organisation of companies or partnerships; and
   (e)   any term incorporated in order to comply with or which reflects—
      (i)   statutory or regulatory provisions of the United Kingdom; or
      (ii)   the provisions or principles of international conventions to which the member States or the Community are party.

### SCHEDULE 2    ASSESSMENT OF GOOD FAITH          Regulation 4(3).

In making an assessment of good faith, regard shall be had in particular to—
   (a)   the strength of the bargaining positions of the parties;

(b)   whether the consumer had an inducement to agree to the term;

(c)   whether the goods or services were sold or supplied to the special order of the consumer, and

(d)   the extent to which the seller or supplier has dealt fairly and equitably with the consumer.

## SCHEDULE 3   INDICATIVE AND ILLUSTRATIVE LIST OF TERMS WHICH MAY BE REGARDED
## AS UNFAIR                            Regulation 4(4).

1.   Terms which have the object or effect of—

(a)   excluding or limiting the legal liability of a seller or supplier in the event of the death of a consumer or personal injury to the latter resulting from an act or omission of that seller or supplier;

(b)   inappropriately excluding or limiting the legal rights of the consumer *vis-à-vis* the seller or supplier or another party in the event of total or partial non-performance or inadequate performance by the seller or supplier of any of the contractual obligations, including the option of offsetting a debt owed to the seller or supplier against any claim which the consumer may have against him;

(c)   making an agreement binding on the consumer whereas provision of services by the seller or supplier is subject to a condition whose realisation depends on his own will alone;

(d)   permitting the seller or supplier to retain sums paid by the consumer where the latter decides not to conclude or perform the contract, without providing for the consumer to receive compensation of an equivalent amount from the seller or supplier where the latter is the party cancelling the contract;

(e)   requiring any consumer who fails to fulfil his obligation to pay a disproportionately high sum in compensation;

(f)   authorising the seller or supplier to dissolve the contract on a discretionary basis where the same facility is not granted to the consumer, or permitting the seller or supplier to retain the sums paid for services not yet supplied by him where it is the seller or supplier himself who dissolves the contract;

(g)   enabling the seller or supplier to terminate a contract of indeterminate duration without reasonable notice except where there are serious grounds for doing so;

(h)   automatically extending a contract of fixed duration where the consumer does not indicate otherwise, when the deadline fixed for the consumer to express this desire not to extend the contract is unreasonably early;

(i)   irrevocably binding the consumer to terms with which he had no real opportunity of becoming acquainted before the conclusion of the contract;

(j)   enabling the seller or supplier to alter the terms of the contract unilaterally without a valid reason which is specified in the contract;

(k)   enabling the seller or supplier to alter unilaterally without a valid reason any characteristics of the product or service to be provided;

(l)   providing for the price of goods to be detemiined at the time of delivery or allowing a seller of goods or supplier of services to increase their price without in both cases giving the consumer the corresponding right to cancel the contract if the final price is too high in relation to the price agreed when the contract was concluded;

(m)   giving the seller or supplier the right to determine whether the goods or services supplied are in conformity with the contract, or giving him the exclusive right to interpret any term of the contract;

(n)   limiting the seller's or supplier's obligation to respect commitments undertaken by his agents or making his commitments subject to compliance with a particular formality;

(o)   obliging the consumer to fulfil all his obligations where the seller or supplier does not perform his;

(p)   giving the seller or supplier the possibility of transferring his rights and obligations under the contract, where this may serve to reduce the guarantees for the consumer, without the latter's agreement;

(q)   excluding or hindering the consumer's right to take legal action or exercise any other legal remedy, particularly by requiring the consumer to take disputes exclusively to arbitration not covered by legal provisions, unduly restricting the evidence available to him or imposing on him a burden of proof which, according to the applicable law, should lie with another party to the contract.

**2.**   Scope of subparagraphs 1(g), (j) and (l)

(a)   Subparagraph 1(g) is without hindrance to terms by which a supplier of financial services reserves the right to terminate unilaterally a contract of indeterminate duration without notice where there is a valid reason, provided that the supplier is required to inform the other contracting party or parties thereof immediately.

(b)   Subparagraph 1(j) is without hindrance to terms under which a supplier of financial services reserves the right to alter the rate of interest payable by the consumer or due to the latter, or the amount of other charges for financial services without notice where there is a valid reason, provided that the supplier is required to inform the other contracting party or parties thereof at the earliest opportunity and that the latter are free to dissolve the contract immediately.

Subparagraph 1(j) is also without hindrance to terms under which a seller or supplier reserves the right to alter unilaterally the conditions of a contract of indeterminate duration, provided that he is required to inform the consumer with reasonable notice and that the consumer is free to disssolve the contract.

(c)   Subparagraphs 1(g), (j) and (l) do not apply to:

— transactions in transferable securities, financial instruments and other products or services where the price is linked to fluctuations in a stock exchange quotation or index or a financial market rate that the seller or supplier does not control;

— contracts for the purchase or sale of foreign currency, traveller's cheques or international money orders denominated in foreign currency;

(d)   Subparagraph 1(l) is without hindrance to price indexation clauses, where lawful, provided that the method by which prices vary is explicitly described.

# Appendix 5

---

# Text of the Unfair Terms in Consumer Contracts Directive

COUNCIL DIRECTIVE 93/13/EEC
of 5 April 1993
on unfair terms in consumer contracts

THE COUNCIL OF THE EUROPEAN COMMUNITIES,
    Having regard to the Treaty establishing the European Economic Community, and in particular Article 100A thereof,
    Having regard to the proposal from the Commission,[1]
    In cooperation with the European Parliament,[2]
    Having regard to the opinion of the Economic and Social Committee,[3]
    Whereas it is necessary to adopt measures with the aim of progressively establishing the internal market before 31 December 1992; whereas the internal market comprises an area without internal frontiers in which goods, persons, services and capital move freely;
    Whereas the laws of Member States relating to the terms of contract between the seller of goods or supplier of services, on the one hand, and the consumer of them, on the other hand, show many disparities, with the result that the national markets for the sale of goods and services to consumers differ from each other and that distortions of competition may arise amongst the sellers and suppliers, notably when they sell and supply in other Member States;

---

[1] OJ No. C 73, 24.3.1992, p. 7.
[2] OJ No. C 326, 16.12.1991, p. 108 and OJ No. C 21, 25.1.1993.
[3] OJ No. C 159, 17.6.1991, p. 34.

Whereas, in particular, the laws of Member States relating to unfair terms in consumer contracts show marked divergences;

Whereas it is the responsibility of the Member States to ensure that contracts concluded with consumers do not contain unfair terms;

Whereas, generally speaking, consumers do not know the rules of law which, in Member States other than their own, govern contracts for the sale of goods or services; whereas this lack of awareness may deter them from direct transactions for the purchase of goods or services in another Member State;

Whereas, in order to facilitate the establishment of the internal market and to safeguard the citizen in his role as consumer when acquiring goods and services under contracts which are governed by the laws of Member States other than his own, it is essential to remove unfair terms from those contracts;

Whereas sellers of goods and suppliers of services will thereby be helped in their task of selling goods and supplying services, both at home and throughout the internal market; whereas competition will thus be stimulated, so contributing to increased choice for Community citizens as consumers;

Whereas the two Community programmes for a consumer protection and information policy[4] underlined the importance of safeguarding consumers in the matter of unfair terms of contract; whereas this protection ought to be provided by laws and regulations which are either harmonized at Community level or adopted directly at that level;

Whereas in accordance with the principle laid down under the heading 'Protection of the economic interests of the consumers', as stated in those programmes: 'acquirers of goods and services should be protected against the abuse of power by the seller or supplier, in particular against one-sided standard contracts and the unfair exclusion of essential rights in contracts';

Whereas more effective protection of the consumer can be achieved by adopting uniform rules of law in the matter of unfair terms; whereas those rules should apply to all contracts concluded between sellers or suppliers and consumers; whereas as a result *inter alia* contracts relating to employment, contracts relating to succession rights, contracts relating to rights under family law and contracts relating to the incorporation and organization of companies or partnership agreements must be excluded from this Directive;

Whereas the consumer must receive equal protection under contracts concluded by word of mouth and written contracts regardless, in the latter case, of whether the terms of the contract are contained in one or more documents;

---

[4] OJ No. C 92, 25.4.1975, p. 1 and OJ No. C 133, 3.6.1981, p. 1.

Whereas, however, as they now stand, national laws allow only partial harmonization to be envisaged; whereas, in particular, only contractual terms which have not been individually negotiated are covered by this Directive; whereas Member States should have the option, with due regard for the Treaty, to afford consumers a higher level of protection through national provisions that are more stringent than those of this Directive;

Whereas the statutory or regulatory provisions of the Member States which directly or indirectly determine the terms of consumer contracts are presumed not to contain unfair terms; whereas, therefore, it does not appear to be necessary to subject the terms which reflect mandatory statutory or regulatory provisions and the principles or provisions of international conventions to which the Member States or the Community are party; whereas in that respect the wording 'mandatory statutory or regulatory provisions' in Article 1(2) also covers rules which, according to the law, shall apply between the contracting parties provided that no other arrangements have been established;

Whereas Member States must however ensure that unfair terms are not included, particularly because this Directive also applies to trades, business or professions of a public nature;

Whereas it is necessary to fix in a general way the criteria for assessing the unfair character of contract terms;

Whereas the assessment, according to the general criteria chosen, of the unfair character of terms, in particular in sale or supply activities of a public nature providing collective services which take account of solidarity among users, must be supplemented by a means of making an overall evaluation of the different interests involved; whereas this constitutes the requirement of good faith; whereas, in making an assessment of good faith, particular regard shall be had to the strength of the bargaining positions of the parties, whether the consumer had an inducement to agree to the term and whether the goods or services were sold or supplied to the special order of the consumer; whereas the requirement of good faith may be satisfied by the seller or supplier where he deals fairly and equitably with the other party whose legitimate interests he has to take into account;

Whereas, for the purposes of this Directive, the annexed list of terms can be of indicative value only and, because of the cause of the minimal character of the Directive, the scope of these terms may be the subject of amplification or more restrictive editing by the Member States in their national laws;

Whereas the nature of goods or services should have an influence on assessing the unfairness of contractual terms;

Whereas, for the purposes of this Directive, assessment of unfair character shall not be made of terms which describe the main subject matter of the contract nor the quality/price ratio of the goods or services supplied; whereas the main subject-matter of the contract and the price/quality ratio may nevertheless be taken into account in assessing the fairness of other terms; whereas it follows, *inter alia*, that in insurance contracts, the terms which clearly define or circumscribe the insured risk and the insurer's liability shall not be subject to such assessment since these restrictions are taken into account in calculating the premium paid by the consumer;

Whereas contracts should be drafted in plain, intelligible language, the consumer should actually be given an opportunity to examine all the terms and, if in doubt, the interpretation most favourable to the consumer should prevail;

Whereas Member States should ensure that unfair terms are not used in contracts concluded with consumers by a seller or supplier and that if, nevertheless, such terms are so used, they will not bind the consumer, and the contract will continue to bind the parties upon those terms if it is capable of continuing in existence without the unfair provisions;

Whereas there is a risk that, in certain cases, the consumer may be deprived of protection under this Directive by designating the law of a non-Member country as the law applicable to the contract; whereas provisions should therefore be included in this Directive designed to avert this risk;

Whereas persons or organizations, if regarded under the law of a Member State as having a legitimate interest in the matter, must have facilities for initiating proceedings concerning terms of contract drawn up for general use in contracts concluded with consumers, and in particular unfair terms, either before a court or before an administrative authority competent to decide upon complaints or to initiate appropriate legal proceedings; whereas this possibility does not, however, entail prior verification of the general conditions obtaining in individual economic sectors;

Whereas the courts or administrative authorities of the Member States must have at their disposal adequate and effective means of preventing the continued application of unfair terms in consumer contracts,

HAS ADOPTED THIS DIRECTIVE:

**Article 1**

1.   The purpose of this Directive is to approximate the laws, regulations and administrative provisions of the Member States relating to unfair terms in contracts concluded between a seller or supplier and a consumer.

2.   The contractual terms which reflect mandatory statutory or regulatory provisions and the provisions or principles of international conventions to which the Member States or the Community are party, particularly in the transport area, shall not be subject to the provisions of this Directive.

### Article 2

For the purposes of this Directive:

    (a)   'unfair terms' means the contractual terms defined in Article 3;

    (b)   'consumer' means any natural person who, in contracts covered by this Directive, is acting for purposes which ae outside his trade, business or profession;

    (c)   'seller or supplier' means any natural or legal person who, in contracts covered by this Directive, is acting for purposes relating to his trade, business or profession, whether publicly owned or privately owned.

### Article 3

1.   A contractual term which has not been individually negotiated shall be regarded as unfair if, contrary to the requirement of good faith, it causes a significant imbalance in the parties' rights and obligations arising under the contract, to the detriment of the consumer.

2.   A term shall always be regarded as not individually negotiated where it has been drafted in advance and the consumer has therefore not been able to influence the substance of the term, particularly in the context of a pre-formulated standard contract

The fact that certain aspects of a term or one specific term have been individually negotiated shall not exclude the application of this Article to the rest of a contract if an overall assessment of the contract indicates that it is nevertheless a pre-formulated standard contract.

Where any seller or supplier claims that a standard term has been individually negotiated, the burden of proof in this respect shall be incumbent on him.

3.   The Annex shall contain an indicative and non-exhaustive list of the terms which may be regarded as unfair.

### Article 4

1.   Without prejudice to Article 7, the unfairness of a contractual term shall be assessed, taking into account the nature of the goods or services for which the contract was concluded and by referring, at the time of conclusion of the contract, to all the circumstances attending the conclusion of the contract and to all the other terms of the contract or of another contract on which it is dependent.

2.   Assessment of the unfair nature of the terms shall relate neither to the definition of the main subject-matter of the contract nor to the adequacy of the price and remuneration, on the one hand, as against the services or goods supplied in exchange, on the other, insofar as these terms are in plain intelligible language.

## Article 5

In the case of contracts where all or certain terms offered to the consumer are in writing, these terms must always be drafted in plain, intelligible language. Where there is doubt about the meaning of a term, the interpretation most favourable to the consumer shall prevail. This rule on interpretation shall not apply in the context of the procedures laid down in Article 7(2).

## Article 6

1.   Member States shall lay down that unfair terms used in a contract concluded with a consumer by a seller or supplier shall, as provided for under their national law, not be binding on the consumer and that the contract shall continue to bind the parties upon those terms if it is capable of continuing in existence without the unfair terms.

2.   Member States shall take the necessary measures to ensure that the consumer does not lose the protection granted by this Directive by virtue of the choice of the law of a non-Member country as the law applicable to the contract if the latter has a close connection with the territory of the Member States.

## Article 7

1.   Member States shall ensure that, in the interests of consumers and of competitors, adequate and effective means exist to prevent the continued use of unfair terms in contracts concluded with consumers by sellers or suppliers.

2.   The means referred to in paragraph 1 shall include provisions whereby persons or organizations, having a legitimate interest under national law in protecting consumers, may take action according to the national law concerned before the courts or before competent administrative bodies for a decision as to whether contractual terms drawn up for general use are unfair, so that they can apply appropriate and effective means to prevent the continued use of such terms.

3.   With due regard for national laws, the legal remedies referred to in paragraph 2 may be directed separately or jointly against a number of sellers or suppliers from the same economic sector or their associations which use or recommend the use of the same general contractual terms or similar terms.

## Article 8

Member States may adopt or retain the most stringent provisions compatible with the Treaty in the area covered by this Directive, to ensure a maximum degree of protection for the consumer.

## Article 9

The Commission shall present a report to the European Parliament and to the Council concerning the application of this Directive five years at the latest after the date in Article 10(1).

**Article 10**

1.  Member States shall bring into force the laws, regulations and administrative provisions necessary to comply with this Directive no later than 31 December 1994. They shall forthwith inform the Commission thereof.

These provisions shall be applicable to all contracts concluded after 31 December 1994.

2.  When Member States adopt these measures, they shall contain a reference to this Directive or shall be accompanied by such reference on the occasion of their official publication. The methods of making such a reference shall be laid down by the Member States.

3.  Member States shall communicate the main provisions of national law which they adopt in the field covered by this Directive to the Commission.

**Article 11**

This Directive is addressed to the Member States.

Done at Luxembourg, 5 April 1993.

*For the Council*
*The President*
N. HELVEG PETERSEN

ANNEX   TERMS REFERRED TO IN ARTICLE 3(3)

1.  **Terms which have the object or effect of:**

(a)   excluding or limiting the legal liability of a seller or supplier in the event of the death of a consumer or personal injury to the latter resulting from an act or omission of that seller or supplier;

(b)   inappropriately excluding or limiting the legal rights of the consumer *vis-à-vis* the seller or supplier or another party in the event of total or partial non-performanc or inadequate performance by the seller or supplier of any of the contractual obligations, including the option of offsetting a debt owed to the seller or supplier against any claim which the consumer may have against him;

(c)   making an agreement binding on the consumer whereas provision of services by the seller or supplier is subject to a condition whose realization depends on his own will alone;

(d)   permitting the seller or supplier to retain sums paid by the consumer where the latter decides not to conclude or perform the contract, without providing for the consumer to receive compensation of an equivalent amount from the seller or supplier where the latter is the party cancelling the contract;

(e)   requiring any consumer who fails to fulfil his obligation to pay a disproportionately high sum in compensation;

(f)   authorizing the seller or supplier to dissolve the contract on a discretionary basis where the same facility is not granted to the consumer, or permitting the seller or supplier to retain the sums paid for services not yet supplied by him where it is the seller or supplier himself who dissolves the contract;

(g)   enabling the seller or supplier to terminate a contract of indeterminate duration without reasonable notice except where there are serious grounds for doing so;

(h)   automatically extending a contract of fixed duration where the consumer does not indicate otherwise, when the deadline fixed for the consumer to express this desire not to extend the contract is unreasonably early;

(i)   irrevocably binding the consumer to terms with which he had no real opportunity of becoming acquainted before the conclusion of the contract;

(j)   enabling the seller or supplier to alter the terms of the contract unilaterally without a valid reason which is specified in the contract;

(k)   enabling the seller or supplier to alter unilaterally without a valid reason any characteristics of the product or service to be provided;

(l)   providing for the price of goods to be determined at the time of delivery or allowing a seller of goods or supplier of services to increase their price without in both cases giving the consumer the corresponding right to cancel the contract if the final price is too high in relation to the price agreed when the contract was concluded;

(m)   giving the seller or supplier the right to determine whether the goods or services supplied are in conformity with the contract, or giving him the exclusive right to interpret any term of the contract;

(n)   limiting the seller's or supplier's obligation to respect commitments undertaken by his agents or making his commitments subject to compliance with a particular formality;

(o)   obliging the consumer to fulfil all his obligations where the seller or supplier does not perform his;

(p)   giving the seller or supplier the possibility of transferring his rights and obligations under the contract, where this may serve to reduce the guarantees for the consumer, without the latter's agreement;

(q)   excluding or hindering the consumer's right to take legal action or exercise any other legal remedy, particularly by requiring the consumer to take disputes exclusively to arbitration not covered by legal provisions, unduly restricting the evidence available to him or imposing on him a burden of proof which, according to the applicable law, should lie with another party to the contract.

## 2.  Scope of subparagraphs (g), (j) and (l)

(a)   Subparagraph (g) is without hindrance to terms by which a supplier of financial services reserves the right to terminate unilaterally a contract of indeterminate duration without notice where there is a valid reason, provided that the supplier is required to inform the other contracting party or parties thereof immediately.

(b)   Subparagraph (j) is without hindrance to terms under which a supplier of financial services reserves the right to alter the rate of interest payable by the consumer or due to the latter, or the amount of other charges for financial services without notice where there is a valid reason, provided that the supplier is required to inform the other contracting party or parties thereof at the earliest opportunity and that the latter are free to dissolve the contract immediately.

Subparagraph (j) is also without hindrance to terms under which a seller or supplier reserves the right to alter unilaterally the conditions of a contract of indeterminate duration, provided that he is required to inform the consumer with reasonable notice and that the consumer is free to dissolve the contract.

(c)   Subparagraphs (g), (j) and (l) do not apply to:

— transactions in transferable securities, financial instruments and other products or services where the price is linked to fluctuations in a stock exchange quotation or index or a financial market rate that the seller or supplier does not control;

— contracts for the purchase or sale of foreign currency, traveller's cheques or international money orders denominated in foreign currency;

(d)   Subparagraph (l) is without hindrance to price-indexation clauses, where lawful, provided that the method by which prices vary is explicitly described.

# Appendix 6

---

# Text of the General Product Safety Regulations 1994

SI 1994/2328

| | |
|---|---|
| *Made* | *5th September 1994* |
| *Laid before Parliament* | *8th September 1994* |
| *Coming into force* | *3rd October 1994* |

Whereas the Secretary of State is a Minister designated[1] for the purposes of section 2(2) of the European Communities Act 1972 in relation to measures relating to consumer protection as regards general product safety;

Now, the Secretary of State, in exercise of the powers conferred on him by section 2(2) of that Act and of all other powers enabling him in that behalf hereby makes the following Regulations:—

## Citation and commencement

1.   These Regulations may be cited as the General Product Safety Regulations 1994 and shall come into force on 3rd October 1994.

## Interpretation

2.—(1)   In these Regulations—

'the 1968 Act' means the Medicines Act 1968;

'the 1987 Act' means the Consumer Protection Act 1987;

'the 1990 Act' means the Food Safety Act 1990;

'commercial activity' includes a business and a trade;

'consumer' means a consumer acting otherwise than in the course of a commercial activity;

---

[1] S.I. 1993/2661.

'dangerous product' means any product other than a safe product;

'distributor' means any professional in the supply chain whose activity does not affect the safety properties of a product;

'enforcement authority' means the Secretary of State, any other Minister of the Crown in charge of a Government Department, any such department and any authority, council and other person on whom functions under these Regulations are imposed by or under regulation 11;

'general safety requirement' means the requirement in regulation 7;

'the GPS Directive' means Council Directive 92/59/EEC on general product safety;[2]

'the 1991 Order' means the Food Safety (Northern Ireland) Order 1991;

'producer' means

(a)   the manufacturer of the product, when he is established in the Commnunity, and includes any person presenting himself as the manufacturer by affixing to the product his name, trade mark or other distinctive mark, or the person who reconditions the product;

(b)   when the manufacturer is not established in the Community—

(i)   if the manufacturer does not have a representative established in the Community, the importer of the product;

(ii)   in all other cases, the manufacturer's representative; and

(c)   other professionals in the supply chain, insofar as their activities may affect the safety properties of a product placed on the market;

'product' means any product intended for consumers or likely to be used by consumers, supplied whether for consideration or not in the course of a commercial activity and whether new, used or reconditioned; provided, however, a product which is used exclusively in the context of a commercial activity even if it is used for or by a consumer shall not be regarded as a product for the purposes of these Regulations provided always and for the avoidance of doubt this exception shall not extend to the supply of such a product to a consumer;

'safe product' means any product which, under normal or reasonably foreseeable conditions of use, including duration, does not present any risk or only the minimum risks compatible with the product's use, considered as acceptable and consistent with a high level of protection for the safety and health of persons, taking into account in particular—

(a)   the characteristics of the product, including its composition, packaging, instructions for assembly and maintenance;

(b)   the effect on other products, where it is reasonably foreseeable that it will be used with other products;

---

[2] OJ No. L 228, 11.8.92, p. 24. [See appendix 7.]

(c)   the presentation of the product, the labelling, any instructions for its use and disposal and any other indication or information provided by the producer; and

(d)   the categories of consumers at serious risk when using the product, in particular children,

and the fact that higher levels of safety may be obtained or other products presenting a lesser degree of risk may be available shall not of itself cause the product to be considered other than a safe product.

(2)   References in these Regulations to the 'Community' are references to the European Economic Area established under the Agreement signed at Oporto on 2nd May 1992 as adjusted by the Protocol signed at Brussels on 17th March 1993.[3]

## Application and revocation

3.   These Regulations do not apply to—

(a)   second-hand products which are antiques;

(b)   products supplied for repair or reconditioning before use, provided the supplier clearly informs the person to whom he supplies the product to that effect; or

(c)   any product where there are specific provisions in rules of Community law governing all aspects of the safety of the product.

4.   The requirements of these Regulations apply to a product where the product is the subject of provisions of Community law other than the GPS Directive insofar as those provisions do not make specific provision governing an aspect of the safety of the product.

5.   For the purposes of these Regulations the provisions of section 10 of the 1987 Act to the extent that they impose general safety requirements which must be complied with if products are to be—

(i)   placed on the market, offered or ageed to be placed on the market or exposed or possessed to be placed on the market by producers; or

(ii)   supplied, offered or agreed to be supplied or exposed or possessed to be supplied by distributors,

are hereby disapplied.

6.—(1)   Sub-paragraph (ii) of paragraph (b) of sub-section (3) of section 10 of the 1987 Act is hereby repealed.

(2)   The Approval of Safety Standards Regulations 1987 are hereby revoked.

---

[3] Protocol 47 and certain Annexes to the Agreement were amended by Decision No. 7/94 of the EEA Joint Committee, which came into force on 1st July 1994 (OJ No. L 160, 28.6.94, p. 1). Council Directive 92/59/EEC was added to Chapter XIX of Annex II to the EEA Agreement by item N in Annex 3 to the said Decision No. 7/94.

**General safety requirement**
**7.** No producer shall place a product on the market unless the product is a safe product.

**Requirement as to information**
**8.**—(1)   Within the limits of his activity, a producer shall—

(a)   provide consumers with the relevant information to enable them to assess the risks inherent in a product throughout the normal or reasonably foreseeable period of its use, where such risks are not immediately obvious without adequate warnings, and to take precautions against those risks; and

(b)   adopt measures commensurate with the characteristics of the products which he supplies, to enable him to be informed of the risks which these products might present and to take appropriate action, including, if necessary, withdrawing the product in question from the market to avoid those risks.

(2)   The measures referred to in sub-paragraph (b) of paragraph (1) above may include, whenever appropriate—

(i)   marking of the products or product batches in such a way that they can be identified;

(ii)   sample testing of marketed products;

(iii)   investigating complaints; and

(iv)   keeping distributors informed of such monitoring.

**Requirements of distributors**
**9.**   A distributor shall act with due care in order to help ensure compliance with the requirements of regulation 7 above and, in particular, without limiting the generality of the foregoing—

(a)   a distributor shall not supply products to any person which he knows, or should have presumed, on the basis of the information in his possession and as a professional, are dangerous products; and

(b)   within the limits of his activities, a distributor shall participate in monitoring the safety of products placed on the market, in particular by passing on information on the product risks and cooperating in the action taken to avoid those risks.

**Presumption of conformity and product assessment**
**10.**—(1)   Where in relation to any product such product conforms to the specific rules of the law of the United Kingdom laying down the health and safety requirements which the product must satisfy in order to be marketed there shall be a presumption that, until the contrary is proved, the product is a safe product.

(2) Where no specific rules as are mentioned or referred to in paragraph (1) exist, the conformity of a product to the general safety requirement shall be assessed taking into account—

      (i)     voluntary national standards of the United Kingdom giving effect to a European standard; or

      (ii)    Community technical specifications; or

      (iii)   if there are no such voluntary national standards of the United Kingdom or Community technical specifications—

          (aa)    standards drawn up in the United Kingdom; or

          (bb)    the codes of good practice in respect of health and safety in the product sector concerned; or

          (cc)    the state of the art and technology

and the safety which consumers may reasonably expect.

### Enforcement

**11.** For the purposes of providing for the enforcement of these Regulations—

      (a)    section 13 of the 1987 Act (prohibition notices and notices to warn) shall (to the extent that it does not already do so) apply to products as it applies to relevant goods under that section;

      (b)    the requirements of these Regulations shall constitute safety provisions for the purposes of sections 14 (suspension notices), 15 (appeals against suspension notices), 16 (forfeiture: England, Wales and Northern Ireland), 17 (forfeiture: Scotland) and 18 (power to obtain information) of the 1987 Act;

      (c)    (i)    subject to paragraph (ii) below a weights and measures authority in Great Britain and a district council in Northern Ireland shall have the same duty to enforce these Regulations as they have in relation to Part II of the 1987 Act, and Part IV, sections 37 and 38 and subsections (3) and (4) of section 42 of that Act shall apply accordingly;

          (ii)    without prejudice to the provisions of paragraphs (a) and (b) above and sub-paragraph (i) above, insofar as these Regulations apply:—

          (aa)   to products licensed in accordance with the provisions of the 1968 Act, it shall be the duty of the enforcement authority as defined in section 132(1) of the 1968 Act to enforce or to secure the enforcement of these Regulations and sections 108 to 115 and section 119 of and Schedule 3 to that Act shall apply accordingly as if these Regulations were regulations made under the said Act;

          (bb)   in relation to food within the meaning of section 1 of the 1990 Act, it shall be the duty of each food authority as defined in section 5 of the 1990 Act to enforce or to secure the enforcement of these Regulations, within its area, in Great Britain and sections 9, 29, 30 and 32 of that Act shall apply accordingly as if these Regulations were food safety requirements made under the said Act and section 10 of that Act shall apply as if these Regulations were regulations made under Part II of that Act; and

(cc)   in relation to food within the meaning of article 2 of the 1991 Order, it shall be the duty of the relevant enforcement authority as provided for in article 26 of that Order to enforce or to secure enforcement of these Regulations in Northern Ireland and articles 8, 29, 30, 31 and 33 of that Order shall apply accordingly as if these Regulations were food safety requirements made under that Order and article 9 of that Order shall apply as if these Regulations were regulations made under Part II of that Order;

(d)   in sections 13(4) and 14(6) of the 1987 Act for the words 'six months' there shall be substituted 'three months'; and

(e)   nothing in this regulation shall authorise any enforcement authority to bring proceedings in Scotland for an offence.

### Offences and preparatory acts

**12.**   Any person who contravenes regulation 7 or 9(a) shall be guilty of an offence.

**13.**   No producer or distributor shall—

(a)   offer or agree to place on the market any dangerous product or expose or possess any such product for placing on the market; or

(b)   offer or agree to supply any dangerous product or expose or possess any such product for supply,

and any person who contravenes the requirements of this regulation shall be guilty of an offence.

### Defence of due diligence

**14.**—(1)   Subject to the following paragraphs of this regulation, in proceedings against any person for an offence under these Regulations it shall be a defence for that person to show that he took all reasonable steps and exercised all due diligence to avoid committing the offence.

(2)   Where in any proceedings against any person for such an offence the defence provided by paragraph (1) above involves an allegation that the commission of the offence was due—

(a)   to the act or default of another, or

(b)   to reliance on information given by another,

that person shall not, without leave of the court, be entitled to rely on the defence unless, not less than seven days before, in England, Wales and Northern Ireland, the hearing of the proceedings or, in Scotland, the trial diet, he has served a notice under paragraph (3) below on the person bringing the proceedings.

(3)   A notice under this paragraph shall give such information identifying or assisting in the identification of the person who committed the act or default or gave the information as is in the possession of the person serving the notice at the time he serves it.

(4)   It is hereby declared that a person shall not be entitled to rely on the defence provided in paragraph (1) above by reason of his reliance on information supplied by another, unless he shows that it was reasonable in all the circumstances for him to have relied on the information, having regard in particular—

   (a)   to the steps which he took, and those which might reasonably have been taken, for the purpose of verifying the information; and

   (b)   to whether he had any reason to disbelieve the information.

(5)   It is hereby declared that a person shall not be entitled to rely on the defence provided by paragraph (1) above or by section 39(1) of the 1987 Act (defence of due diligence) if he has contravened regulation 9(b).

**Liability of persons other than principal offender**

**15.**—(1)   Where the commission by any person of an offence to which regulation 14 above applies is due to the act or default committed by some other person in the course of a commercial activity of his, the other person shall be guilty of an offence and may be proceeded against and punished by virtue of this paragraph whether or not proceedings are taken against the first-mentioned person.

(2)   Where a body corporate is guilty of an offence under these Regulations (including where it is so guilty by virtue of paragraph (1) above) in respect of any act or default which is shown to have been committed with the consent or connivance of, or to be attributable to any neglect on the part of any director, manager, secretary or other similar officer of the body corporate or any person who was purporting to act in any such capacity he, as well as the body corporate, shall be guilty of that offence and shall be liable to be proceeded against and punished accordingly.

(3)   Where the affairs of a body corporate are managed by its members, paragraph (2) above shall apply in relation to the acts and defaults of a member in connection with his functions of management as if he were a director of the body corporate.

(4)   Where a Scottish partnership is guilty of an offence under regulation 14 above (including where it is so guilty by virtue of paragraph (1) above) in respect of any act or default which is shown to have been committed with the consent or connivance of, or to be attributable to any neglect on the part of, a partner in the partnership, he, as well as the partnership, shall be guilty of that offence and shall be liable to be proceeded against and punished accordingly.

### Extension of the time for bringing summary proceedings

**16.**—(1)   Notwithstanding section 127 of the Magistrates' Courts Act 1980 and article 19 of the Magistrates' Courts (Northern Ireland) Order 1981, in England, Wales and Northern Ireland a magistrates' court may try an information (in the case of England and Wales) or a complaint (in the case of Northern Ireland) in respect of proceedings for an offence under regulation 12 or 13 above if (in the case of England and Wales) the information is laid or (in the case of Northern Ireland) the complaint is made within twelve months from the date of the offence.

(2)   Notwithstanding section 331 of the Criminal Procedure (Scotland) Act 1975, in Scotland sumary proceedings for an offence under regulation 12 or 13 above may be commenced at any time within twelve months from the date of the offence.

(3)   For the purposes of paragraph (2) above, section 331(3) of the Criminal Procedure (Scotland) Act 1975 shall apply as it applies for the purposes of that section.

### Penalties

**17.**   A person guilty of an offence under regulation 12 or 13 above shall be liable on summary conviction to—

(a)   imprisonment for a term not exceeding three months; or

(b)   a fine not exceeding level 5 on the standard scale;

or to both.

### Duties of enforcement authorities

**18.**—(1)   Every enforcement authority shall give immediate notice to the Secretary of State of any action taken by it to prohibit or restrict the supply of any product or forfeit or do any other thing in respect of any product for the purposes of these Regulations.

(2)   The requirements of paragraph (1) above shall not apply in the case of any action taken in respect of any second-hand product.

*Ferrers*
Minister of State
5th September 1994                                      Department of Trade and Industry

# Appendix 7

# Text of the General Product Safety Directive

### COUNCIL DIRECTIVE 92/59/EEC
### of 29 June 1992
### on general product safety

THE COUNCIL OF THE EUROPEAN COMMUNITIES,

Having regard to the Treaty establishing the European Economic Community, and in particular Article 100a thereof,

Having regard to the proposal from the Commission,[1]

In cooperation with the European Parliament,[2]

Having regard to the opinion of the Economic and Social Committee,[3]

Whereas it is important to adopt measures with the aim of progressively establishing the internal market over a period expiring on 31 December 1992; whereas the internal market is to comprise an area without internal frontiers in which the free movement of goods, persons, services and capital is ensured;

Whereas some Member States have adopted horizontal legislation on product safety, imposing, in particular, a general obligation on economic operators to market only safe products; whereas those legislations differ in the level of protection afforded to persons; whereas such disparities and the absence of horizontal legislation in other Member States are liable to create barriers to trade and distortions of competition within the internal market;

Whereas it is very difficult to adopt Community legislation for every product which exists or may be developed; whereas there is a need for a

---

[1] OJ No. C 156, 27.6.1990, p. 8.
[2] OJ No. C 96, 17.4.1990, p. 283 and Decision of 11 June 1992 (not yet published in the Official Journal).
[3] OJ No. C 75, 26.3.1990, p. 1.

broadly based, legislative framework of a horizontal nature to deal with those products, and also to cover lacunae in existing or forthcoming specific legislation, in particular with a view to ensuring a high level of protection of safety and health of persons, as required by Article 100a(3) of the Treaty;

Whereas it is therefore necessary to establish on a Community level a general safety requirement for any product placed on the market that is intended for consumers or likely to be used by consumers; whereas certain second-hand goods should nevertheless be excluded by their nature;

Whereas production equipment, capital goods and other products used exclusively in the context of a trade or business are not covered by this Directive;

Whereas, in the absence of more specific safety provisions, within the framework of Community regulations, covering the products concerned, the provisions of this Directive are to apply;

Whereas when there are specific rules of Community law, of the total harmonization type, and in particular rules adopted on the basis of the new approach, which lay down obligations regarding product safety, further obligations should not be imposed on economic operators as regards the placing on the market of products covered by such rules;

Whereas, when the provisions of specific Community regulations cover only certain aspects of safety or categories of risks in respect of the product concerned, the obligations of economic operators in respect of such aspects are determined solely by those provisions;

Whereas it is appropriate to supplement the duty to observe the general safety requirement by an obligation on economic operators to supply consumers with relevant information and adopt measures commensurate with the characteristics of the products, enabling them to be informed of the risks that these products might present;

Whereas in the absence of specific regulations, criteria should be defined whereby product safety can be assessed;

Whereas Member States must establish authorities responsible for monitoring product safety and with powers to take the appropriate measures;

Whereas it is necessary in particular for the appropriate measures to include the power for Member States to organize, immediately and efficiently, the withdrawal of dangerous products already placed on the market;

Whereas it is necessary for the preservation of the unity of the market to inform the Commission of any measure restricting the placing on the market of a product or requiring its withdrawal from the market except for those relating to an event which is local in effect and in any case limited to the territory of the Member State concerned; whereas such measures can be taken only in compliance with the provisions of the Treaty, and in particular Articles 30 to 36;

Whereas this Directive applies without prejudice to the notification procedures in Council Directive 83/189/EEC of 28 March 1983 laying down a procedure for the provision of information in the field of technical standards and regulations[4] and in Commission Decision 88/383/EEC of 24 February 1988 providing for the improvement of information on safety, hygiene and health at work;[5]

Whereas effective supervision of product safety requires the setting up at national and Community levels of a system of rapid exchange of information in emergency situations in respect of the safety of a product and whereas the procedure laid down by Council Decision 89/45/EEC of 21 December 1988 on a Community system for the rapid exchange of information on dangers arising from the use of consumer products[6] should therefore be incorporated into this Directive and the above Decision should be repealed; whereas it is also advisable for this Directive to take over the detailed procedures adopted under the above Decision and to give the Commission, assisted by a committee, power to adapt them;

Whereas, moreover, equivalent notification procedures already exist for pharmaceuticals, which come under Directives 75/319/EEC[7] and 81/851/EEC,[8] concerning animal diseases referred to in Directive 82/894/EEC,[9] for products of animal origin covered by Directive 89/662/EEC,[10] and in the form of the system for the rapid exchange of information in radiological emergencies under Decision 87/600/Euratom;[11]

Whereas it is primarily for Member States, in compliance with the Treaty and in particular with Articles 30 to 36 thereof, to take appropriate measures with regard to dangerous products located within their territory;

Whereas in such a situation the decision taken on a particular product could differ from one Member State to another; whereas such a difference may entail unacceptable disparities in consumer protection and constitute a barrier to intra-Community trade;

Whereas it may be necessary to cope with serious product-safety problems which affect or could affect, in the immediate future, all or a large part of the Community and which, in view of the nature of the safety problem posed by the product cannot be dealt with effectively in a manner commensurate with the urgency of the problem under the procedures laid down in the

---

[4] OJ No. L 109, 26.4.1983, p. 8.
[5] OJ No. L 183, 14.7.1988, p. 34.
[6] OJ No. L 17, 21.1.1989, p. 51.
[7] OJ No. L 147, 9.6.1975, p. 13.
[8] OJ No. L 317, 6.11.1981, p. 1.
[9] OJ No. L 378, 31.12.1982, p. 58.
[10] OJ No. L 395, 30.12.1989, p. 13.
[11] OJ No. L 371, 30.12.1987, p. 76.

specific rules of Community law applicable to the products or category of products in question;

Whereas it is therefore necessary to provide for an adequate mechanism allowing, in the last resort, for the adoption of measures applicable throughout the Community, in the form of a decision addressed to the Member States, in order to cope with emergency situations as mentioned above; whereas such a decision is not of direct application to economic operators and must be incorporated into a national instrument; whereas measures adopted under such a procedure can be no more than interim measures that have to be taken by the Commission assisted by a committee of representatives of the Member States; whereas, for reasons of cooperation with the Member States, it is appropriate to provide for a regulatory committee according to procedure III(b) of Decision 87/373/EEC;[12]

Whereas this Directive does not affect victims' rights within the meaning of Council Directive 85/374/EEC of 25 July 1985 on the approximation of the laws, regulations and administrative provisions of the Member States concerning liability for defective products;[13]

Whereas it is necessary that Member States provide for appropriate means of redress before the competent courts in respect of measures taken by the competent authorities which restrict the placing on the market of a product or require its withdrawal;

Whereas it is appropriate to consider, in the light of experience, possible adaptation of this Directive, particularly as regards extension of its scope and provisions on emergency situations and intervention at Community level;

Whereas, in addition, the adoption of measures concerning imported products with a view to preventing risks to the safety and health of persons must comply with the Community's international obligations,

HAS ADOPTED THIS DIRECTIVE:

## TITLE I   Objective — Scope —- Definitions

**Article 1**

1. The purpose of the provisions of this Directive is to ensure that products placed on the market are safe.

2. The provisions of this Directive shall apply insofar as there are no specific provisions in rules of Community law governing the safety of the products concerned.

In particular, where specific rules of Community law contain provisions imposing safety requirements on the products which they govern, the

---

[12] OJ No. L 197, 18.7.1987, p. 33.
[13] OJ No. L 210, 7.8.1985, p. 29.

provisions of Articles 2 to 4 of this Directive shall not, in any event, apply to those products.

Where specific rules of Community law contain provisions governing only certain aspects of product safety or categories of risks for the products concerned, those are the provisions which shall apply to the products concerned with regard io the relevant safety aspects or risks.

## Article 2

For the purposes of this Directive:

(a) *product* shall mean any product intended for consumers or likely to be used by consumers, supplied whether for consideration or not in the course of a commercial activity and whether new, used or reconditioned.
However, this Directive shall not apply to second-hand products supplied as antiques or as products to be repaired or reconditioned prior to being used, provided that the supplier clearly informs the person to whom he supplies the product to that effect;

(b) *safe product* shall mean any product which, under normal or reasonably foreseeable conditions of use, including duration, does not present any risk or only the minimum risks compatible with the product's use, considered as acceptable and consistent with a high level of protection for the safety and health of persons, taking into account the following points in particular:

— the characteristics of the product, including its composition, packaging, instructions for assembly and maintenance,

— the effect on other products, where it is reasonably foreseeable that it will be used with other products,

— the presentation of the product, the labelling, any instructions for its use and disposal and any other indication or information provided by the producer,

— the categories of consumers at serious risk when using the product, in particular children.

The feasibility of obtaining higher levels of safety or the availability of other products presenting a lesser degree of risk shall not constitute grounds for considering a product to be 'unsafe' or 'dangerous';

(c) *dangerous product* shall mean any product which does not meet the defintion of 'safe product' according to point (b) hereof;

(d) *producer* shall mean:

— the manufacturer of the product, when he is established in the Community, and any other person presenting himself as the manufacturer by affixing to the product his name, trade mark or other distinctive mark, or the person who reconditions the product,

— the manufacturer's representative, when the manufacturer is not established in the Community or, if there is no representative established in the Community, the importer of the product,

— other professionals in the supply chain, insofar as their activities may affect the safety properties of a product placed on the market.

(e) *distributor* shall mean any professional in the supply chain whose activity does not affect the safety properties of a product.

## TITLE II    — General safety requirement

### Article 3

1.   Producers shall be obliged to place only safe products on the market.

2.   Within the limits of their respective activities, producers shall:

— provide comumers with the relevant information to enable them to assess the risks inherent in a product throughout the normal or reasonably foreseeable period of its use, where such risks are not immediately obvious without adequate warnings, and to take precautions against those risks.

Provision of such warnings does not, however, exempt any person from compliance with the other requirements laid down in this Directive,

— adopt measures commensurate with the characteristics of the products which they supply, to enable them to be informed of risks which these products might present and to take appropriate action including, if necessary, withdrawing the product in question from the market to avoid these risks.

The above measures shall for example include, whenever appropriate, marking of the products or product batches in such a way that they can be identified, sample testing of marketed products, investigaing complaints made and keeping distributors informed of such monitoring.

3.   Distributors shall be required to act with due care in order to help to ensure compliance with the general safety requirement, in particular by not supplying products which they know or should have presumed, on the basis of the information in their possesion and as professionals, do not comply with this requirement. In particular, within the limits of their respective activities, they shall participate in monitoring the safety of products placed on the market, especially by passing on information on product risks and cooperating in the action taken to avoid these risks.

### Article 4

1.   Where there are no specific Community provisions governing the safety of the products in question, a product shall be deemed safe when it conforms to the specific rules of national law of the Member State in whose territory the product is in circulation, such rules being drawn up in

conformity with the Treaty, and in particular Articles 30 and 36 thereof, and laying down the health and safety requirements which the product must satisfy in order to be marketed.

2.  In the absence of specific rules as referred to in paragraph 1, the conformity of a product to the general safety requirement shall be assessed having regard to voluntary national standards giving effect to a European standard or, where they exist, to Community technical specifications or, failing these, to standards drawn up in the Member State in which the product is in circulation, or to the codes of good practice in respect of health and safety in the sector concerned or to the state of the art and technology and to the safety which consumers may reasonably expect.

3.  Conformity of a product with the provisions mentioned in paragraphs 1 or 2 shall not bar the competent authorities of the Member States from taking appropriate measures to impose restrictions on its being placed on the market or to require its withdrawal from the market where there is evidence that, despite such conformity, it is dangerous to the health and safety of consumers.

TITLE III   Obligations and powers of the Member States

**Article 5**
Member States shall adopt the necessary laws, regulations and administrative provisions to make producers and distributors comply with their obligations under this Directive in such a way that products placed on the market are safe.

In particular, Member States shall establish or nominate authorities to monitor the compliance of products with the obligation to place only safe products on the market and arrange for such authorities to have the necessary powers to take the appropriate measures incumbent upon them under this Directive, including the possibility of imposing suitable penalties in the event of failure to comply with the obligations deriving from this Directive. They shall notify the Commission of the said authorities; the Commission shall pass on the information to the other Member States.

**Article 6**
1.  For the purposes of Article 5, Member States shall have the necessary powers, acting in accordance with the degree of risk and in conformity with the Treaty, and in particular Articles 30 and 36 thereof, to adopt appropriate measures with a view, *inter alia*, to:

(a)   organizing appropriate checks on the safety properties of products, even after their being placed on the market as being safe, on an adequate scale, up to the final stage of use or consumption;

(b)   requiring all necessary information from the parties concerned;

(c)   taking samples of a product or a product line and subjecting them to safety checks;

(d)   subjecting product marketing to prior conditions designed to ensure product safety and requiring that suitable warnings be affixed regarding the risks which the product may present;

(e)   making arrangements to ensure that persons who might be exposed to a risk from a product are informed in good time and in a suitable manner of the said risk by, *inter alia*, the publication of special warnings;

(f)   temporarily prohibiting, for the period required to carry out the various checks, anyone from supplying, offering to supply or exhibiting a product or product batch, whenever there are precise and consistent indications that they are dangerous;

(g)   prohibiting the placing on the market of a product or product batch which has proved dangerous and establishing the accompanying measures needed to ensure that the ban is complied with;

(h)   organizing the effective and immediate withdrawal of a dangerous product or product batch already on the market and, if necessary, its destruction under appropriate conditions.

2.   The measures to be taken by the competent authorities of the Member States under this Article shall be addressed, as appropriate, to:

(a)   the producer;

(b)   within the limits of their respective activities, distributors and in particular the party responsible for the first stage of distribution on the national market;

(c)   any other person, where necessary, with regard to cooperation in action taken to avoid risks arising from a product.

TITLE IV   Notification and exchanges of information

**Article 7**

1.   Where a Member State takes measures which restrict the placing of a product or a product batch on the market or require its withdrawal from the market, such as provided for in Article 6(1)(d) to (h), the Member State shall, to the extent that such notification is not required under any specific Community legislation, inform the Commission of the said measures, specifying its reasons for adopting them. This obligation shall not apply where the measures relate to an event which is local in effect and in any case limited to the territory of the Member State concerned.

2.   The Commission shall enter into consultations with the parties concerned as quickly as possible. Where the Commission concludes, after such consultations, that the measure is justified, it shall immediately inform the

Member State which initiated the action and the other Member States. Where the Commission concludes, after such consultations, that the measure is not justified, it shall immediately inform the Member State which initiated the action.

TITLE V   Emergency situations and action at Community level

### Article 8

1.   Where a Member State adopts or decides to adopt emergency measures to prevent, restrict or impose specific conditions on the possible marketing or use, within its own territory, of a product or product batch by reason of a serious and immediate risk presented by the said product or product batch to the health and safety of consumers, it shall forthwith inform the Commission thereof, unless provision is made for this obligation in procedures of a similar nature in the context of other Community instruments.

This obligation shall not apply if the effects of the risk do not, or cannot, go beyond the territory of the Member State concerned.

Without prejudice to the provisions of the first subparagraph, Member States may pass on to the Commission any information in their possession regarding the existence of a serious and immediate risk before deciding to adopt the measures in question.

2.   On receiving this information, the Commission shall check to see whether it complies with the provisions of this Directive and shall forward it to the other Member States, which, in turn, shall immediately inform the Commission of any measures adopted.

3.   Detailed procedures for the Community information system described in this Article are set out in the Annex. They shall be adopted by the Commission in accordance with the procedure laid down in Article 11.

### Article 9

If the Commission becomes aware, through notification given by the Member States or through information provided by them, in particular under Article 7 or Article 8, of the existence of a serious and immediate risk from a product to the health and safety of consumers in various Member States and if:

(a)   one or more Member States have adopted measures entailing restrictions on the marketing of the product or requiring its withdrawal from the market, such as those in Article 6(1)(d) to (h);

(b)   Member States differ on the adoption of measures to deal with the risk in question;

(c)   the risk cannot be dealt with, in view of the nature of the safety issue posed by the product and in a manner compatible with the urgency of the case, under the other procedures laid down by the specific Community legislation applicable to the product or category of products concerned; and

(d)   the risk can be eliminated effectively only by adopting appropriate measures applicable at Community level, in order to ensure the protection of the health and safety of consumers and the proper functioning of the common market,

the Commission, after consulting the Member States and at the request of at least one of them, may adopt a decision, in accordance with the procedure laid down in Article 11, requiring Member States to take temporary measures from among those listed in Article 6(1)(d) to (h).

## Article 10

1.   The Commission shall be assisted by a Committee on Product Safety Emergencies, hereinafter referred to as 'the Committee', composed of the representatives of the Member States and chaired by a representative of the Commission.

2.   Without prejudice to Article 9(c), there shall be close cooperation between the Committee referred to in paragraph 1 and the other Committees established by specific rules of Community law to assist the Commission as regards the health and safety aspects of the product concerned.

## Article 11

1.   The Commission representative shall submit to the Committee a draft of the measures to be taken. The Committee, having verified that the conditions listed in Article 9 are fulfilled, shall deliver its opinion on the draft within a time limit which the Chairman may lay down according to the urgency of the matter but which may not exceed one month. The opinion shall be delivered by the majority laid down in Article 148(2) of the Treaty for adoption of decisions by the Council on a proposal from the Commission. The votes of the representatives of the Member States within the Committee shall be weighted in the manner set out in that Article. The Chairman shall not vote.

The Commission shall adopt the measures in question, if they are in accordance with the opinion of the Committee. If the measures proposed are not in accordance with the Committee's opinion, or in the absence of an opinion, the Commission shall forthwith submit to the Council a proposal regarding the measures to be taken. The Council shall act by a qualified majority.

If the Council has not acted within 15 days of the date on which the proposal was submitted to it, the measures proposed shall be adopted by the Commission unless the Council has decided against them by a simple majority.

2.   Any measure adopted under this procedure shall be valid for no longer than three months. That period may be prolonged under the same procedure.

3.   Member States shall take all necessary measures to implement the decisions adopted under this procedure within less than 10 days.

4.   The competent authorities of the Member States responsible for carrying out measures adopted under this procedure shall, within one month, give the parties concerned an opportunity to submit their views and shall inform the Commission accordingly.

**Article 12**

The Member States and the Commission shall take the steps necessary to ensure that their officials and agents are required not to disclose information obtained for the purposes of this Directive which, by its nature, is covered by professional secrecy, except for information relating to the safety properties of a given product which must be made public if circumstances so require, in order to protect the health and safety of persons.

TITLE VI   Miscellaneous and final provisions

**Article 13**

This Directive shall be without prejudice to Directive 85/374/EEC.

**Article 14**

1.   Any decision adopted under this Directive and involving restrictions on the placing of a product on the market, or requiring its withdrawal from the market, must state the appropriate reasons on which it is based. It shall be notified as soon as possible to the party concerned and shall indicate the remedies available under the provisions in force in the Member State in question and the time limits applying to such remedies.

The parties concerned shall, whenever feasible, be given an opportunity to submit their views before the adoption of the measure. If this has not been done in advance because of the urgency of the measures to be taken, such opportunity shall be given in due course after the measure has been implemented.

Measures requiring the withdrawal of a product from the market shall take into consideration the need to encourage distributors, users and consumers to contribute to the implementation of such measures.

2.   Member States shall ensure that any measure taken by the competent authorities involving restrictions on the placing of a product on the market or requiring its withdrawal from the market can be challenged before the competent courts.

3.   Any decision taken by virtue of this Directive and involving restrictions on the placing of a product on the market or requiring its withdrawal

from the market shall be entirely without prejudice to assessment of the liability of the party concerned, in the light of the national criminal law applying in the case in question.

### Article 15
Every two years following the date of adoption, the Commission shall submit a report on the implementation of this Directive to the European Parliament and the Council.

### Article 16
Four years from the date referred to in Article 17(1), on the basis of a Commission report on the expperience acquired, together with appropriate proposals, the Council shall decide whether to adjust this Directive, in particular with a view to extending its scope as laid down in Article 1(1) and Article 2(a), and whether the provisions of Title V should be amended.

### Article 17
1.   Member States shall adopt the laws, regulations and administrative provisions necessary to comply with this Directive by 29 June 1994 at the latest. They shall forthwith inform the Commission thereof. The provisions adopted shall apply with effect from 29 June 1994.

2.   When these measures are adopted by the Member States, they shall contain a reference to this Directive or be accompanied by such a reference on the occasion of their official publication. The methods of making such a reference shall be laid down by the Member States.

3.   Member States shall communicate to the Commission the text of the provisions of national law which they adopt in the area covered by this Directive.

### Article 18
Decision 89/45/EEC is hereby repealed on the date referred to in Article 17(1).

### Article 19
This Directive is addresed to the Member States.

Done at Luxembourg, 29 June 1992.

*For the Council*
*The President*
Carlos BORREGO

ANNEX   DETAILED PROCEDURES FOR THE APPLICATION OF THE
COMMUNITY SYSTEM FOR THE RAPID EXCHANGE OF
INFORMATION PROVIDED FOR IN ARTICLE 8

1.   The system covers products placed on the market as defined in Article
2(a) of this Directive.

Pharmaceuticals, which come under Directive 75/319/EEC and 81/851/
EEC, and animals, to which Directive 82/894/EEC applies and products of
animal origin, as far as they are covered by Directive 89/662/EEC, and the
system for radiological emergencies which covers widespread contamination
of products (Decision 87/600/Euratom), are excluded, since they are covered
by equivalent notification procedures.

2.   The system is essentially aimed at a rapid exchange of information in
the event of a serious and immediate risk to the health and safety of
consumers. It is impossible to lay down specific criteria as to what, precisely,
constitutes an immediate and serious risk; in this regard, the national
authorities will therefore judge each individual case on its merits. It should
be noted that, as Article 8 of this Directive relates to immediate threats posed
by a product to consumers, products involving possible long-term risks,
which call for a study of possible technical changes by means of directives
or standards are not concerned.

3.   As soon as a serious and immediate risk is detected, the national
authority shall consult, insofar as possible and appropriate, the producer or
distributor of the product concerned. Their point of view and the details
which they supply may be useful both to the administrations of the Member
States and to the Commission in determining what action should be taken to
ensure that the consumer is protected with a minimum of commercial
disruption. To these ends the Member States should endeavour to obtain the
maximum of information on the products and the nature of the danger,
without compromising the need for rapidity.

4.   As soon as a Member State has detected a serious and immediate risk,
the effects of which extend or could extend beyond its territory, and measures
have been taken or decided on, it shall immediately inform the Commission.
The Member State shall indicate that it is notifying the Commission under
Article 8 of this Directive. All available details shall be given, in particular
on:

   (a)   information to identify the product;

   (b)   the danger involved, including the results of any tests/analyses
which are relevant to assessing the level of risk;

   (c)   the nature of the measures taken or decided on;

   (d)   information on supply chains where such information is possible.

Such information must be transmitted in writing, preferably by telex or fax, but may be preceded by a telephone call to the Commission. It should be remembered that the speed with which the information is communicated is crucial.

5. Without prejudice to point 4, Member States may, where appropriate, pass information to the Commission at the stage preceding the decision on the measures to be taken. Immediate contact, as soon as a risk is discovered or suspected, can in fact facilitate preventive action.

6. If the Member State considers certain information to be confidential, it should specify this and justify its request for confidentiality, bearing in mind that the need to take effective measures to protect consumers normally outweighs considerations of confidentiality. It should also be remembered that precautions are taken in all cases, both by the Commission and by the members of the network responsible in the various Member States, to avoid any unnecessary disclosure of information likely to harm the reputation of a product or series of products.

7. The Commission shall verify the conformity of the information received with Article 8 of this Directive, contact the notifying country, if necessary, and forward the information immediately by telex or fax to the relevant authorities in the other Member States with a copy to each permanent representation; these authorities may, at the same time as the transmission of the telex, be contacted by telephone. The Commission may also contact the Member State presumed to be the country of origin of the product to carry out the necessary verifications.

8. At the same time the Commission, when it considers it to be necessary, and in order to supplement the information received, can in exceptional circumstances institute an investigation of its own motion and/or convene the Committee on Emergencies provided for in Article 10(1) of this Directive.

In the case of such an investigation Member States shall supply the Commission with the requested information to the best of their ability.

9. The other Member States are requested, wherever possible, to inform the Commission without delay of the following:

(a) whether the product has been marketed in its territory;

(b) supplementary information it has obtained on the danger involved, including the results of any tests/analyses carried out to assess the level of risk,

and in any case they must inform the Commission as soon as possible of the following:

(c) the measures taken or decided on, of the type mentioned in Article 8(1) of this Directive;

(d)   when the product mentioned in this information has been found within their territory but no measures have been taken or decided on and the reasons why no measures are to be taken.

10.   The Commission may, in the light of the evolution of a case and the information received from Member States under point 9 above, convene the above Committee on Emergencies in order to exchange views on the results obtained and to evaluate the measures taken. The Committee on Emergencies may also be convened at the request of a representative of a Member State.

11.   The Commission shall, by means of its internal coordination procedures, endeavour to:

(a)   avoid unnecessary duplication in dealing with notifications;

(b)   make full use of the expertise available within the Commission;

(c)   keep the other services concerned fully informed;

(d)   ensure that discussions in the various relevant committees are held in accordance with Article 10 of this Directive.

12.   When a Member State intends, apart from any specific measures taken because of serious and immediate risks, to modify its legislation by adopting technical specifications, the latter must be notified to the Commission at the draft stage, in accordance with Directive 83/189/EEC, if necessary, quoting the urgent reasons set out in Article 9(3) of that Directive.

13.   To allow it to have an overview of the situation, the Committee on Emergencies shall be periodically informed of all the notifications received and of the follow-up. With regard to points 8 and 10 above, and in those cases which fall within the scope of procedures and/or committees provided for by Community legislation governing specific products or product sectors, those committees shall be involved. In cases where the Committee on Emergencies is not involved and no provisions are made under 11(d), the contact points shall be informed of any exchange of views within other committees.

14.   At present there are two networks of contact points: the food products network and the non-food products network. The list of contact points and officials responsible for the networks with telephone, telex and fax numbers and addresses is confidential and distributed to the members of the network only. This list enables contact to be established with the Commission and between Member States in order to facilitate clarification of points of detail. When such contacts between Member States give rise to new information of general interest, the Member States which initiated the bilateral contact shall inform the Commission. Only information received or confirmed through contact points in Member States may be considered as received through the rapid exchange of information procedure.

Every year the Commission shall carry out a review of the effectiveness of the network, of any necessary improvements and of the progress made in the communications technology between the authorities responsible for its operation.

# Index